The Poeming Pigeon
A Literary Journal of Poetry

The Poeming Pigeon
A Literary Journal of Poetry

Volume 1, Issue 2
Poems about Food

A Publication of The Poetry Box®

©2015 The Poetry Box®
All rights reserved.
Each poem copyright reserved by individual authors.
Original Cover Illustration & Photographs by Robert R. Sanders.
Editing & Book Design by Shawn Aveningo.
Cover Design by Robert R. Sanders.
Printed in the United States of America.

No part of this book may be reproduced
in any matter whatsoever without written
permission from the author, except in the case
of brief quotations embodied in critical essays,
reviews and articles.

Library of Congress Control Number: 2015948388

ISBN-13: 978-0-9863304-7-6
ISBN-10: 09863304277

Published by The Poetry Box®, 2015
Beaverton, Oregon
www.ThePoetryBox.com
530.409.0721

*To those working toward creating a world
where people never go hungry*

Contents

Introduction 11
Appetite ~Paulann Petersen 15
Let those love now ~Linda Ferguson 16
The Trouble with Cooking: A Poem of Compulsion ~Jan Duncan-O'Neal 17
A Benediction ~Linda Flaherty Haltmaier 19
The Cheesecake Response ~Lori Loranger 20
Because Throbbing ~A.J. Huffman 21
New Spring Rites ~Rick Blum 23
Pi/Pie ~Jan Haag 24
Sin Eating ~Nathan Tompkins 26
The Surprise Inside the Cake ~Linda Ferguson 27
Cookie-lover ~Boutheina Boughnim Laarif 29
I Never Wanted Dinner ~Debra McQueen 30
Food Calendar Souvenir ~Laurie Kolp 31
Eggs, Three ~Jane Burn 32
Majesty ~Elizabeth Moscoso 33
Lengua ~Judith Skillman 34
An Atlas of Taste ~Paulann Petersen 36
A Reconciliation ~Tammy Robacker 37
Gobstopper ~Heather Angier 38
Looking at Bread ~Penelope Scambly Schott 39
Stock ~Connie Post 41
Chicken Matzo Ball Soup ~Joanne S. Bodin 43
Scars, Phillipine Sweet Potatoes and Mango ~Georgette Howington 44
Sugarloaf ~Jeanine Stevens 45
Apple Strudel ~Paul Belz 46
Plums ~Mariano Zaro 47
Keeping Count ~Rachelle M. Parker 49
Echo ~Christine Easterly 50

Tomatl, Tenochtitlán, Before Cortés ~*Sylvia Riojas Vaughn* 51
Harvest Moon ~*JC Reilly* 52
The Seeds of Thanksgiving ~*Tricia Knoll* 53
Vegetable Soul ~*Mary Kay Rummel* 54
Ode to a Purple Onion ~*Elizabeth Urenios* 55
Massaged Kale Salad ~*Susan Star Paddock* 57
Potato ~*Mark L. Levinson* 58
Radish ~*Joan Colby* 59
Diet ~*Katy Brown* 60
Sunday Brunch ~*Suzanne Bruce* 62
Luaus Are Coconut Scented Shams ~*JenniferAnne Morrison* 64
Buffalo Wild Wings ~*Richard King Perkins II* 65
Al Dente ~*Joan Leotta* 66
The Best Thing About Ketchup ~*Tricia Knoll* 67
Avocado ~*Taylor Graham* 68
Last Suppers ~*Linda Jackson Collins* 69
Grilled Cheese ~*Andrew David Viceroy* 70
Batch Loaves ~*Stephen McGuinness* 71
On Which Side My ~*Dan Raphael* 72
Pickled Beats ~*Cassie Von Alst* 73
Three Months After Her Funeral ~*Lori Levy* 76
The Family Legacy ~*Jane Simpson* 77
My Grandmother Was a Witch ~*Lu Pierro* 78
Bacalao ~*Victorio Reyes* 80
Banana Sandwich ~*Ann Howells* 82
Peanuthead ~*Kimberly White* 83
Cookie Dough (or What Didn't Make Us Sick) ~*Deborah Meltvedt* 85
When Living Well Isn't Enough, Invite Your Enemies
   to Dinner ~*Matt Hohner* 87
Half-past Ennui ~*Sreemoyee Roy Chowdhury* 88
The Corruption of Gazpacho ~*Laurel Feigenbaum* 90

The Grizzly Course ~Karla Linn Merrifield	91
Foodie ~Sarah Ghoshal	92
Crock Pot Cooking in Terza Rima ~Carolyn Martin	93
On the Guilt of Being a Well-Fed Poet ~Claudia F. Savage	94
What the Muse Eats ~Jane Yolen	96
Leftovers ~Ann Privateer	97
A Fly on the Wall Café ~Martie Odell-Ingebretsen	98
In Ghent ~Irene Bloom	99
I stopped by the side of the road ~Christine Kouwenhoven	101
Oh Mango! ~Helen Kerner	102
How to Swallow a Butterfly ~Dawn Orosco	103
How to Eat a Strawberry ~Shawn Aveningo	105
Differences ~Terri Niccum	106
Learning Abandon ~Claudia F. Savage	107
Oyster ~Jeannie E. Roberts	108
Cold Pizza for Breakfast ~Cathy Cain	110
Mushroom Hunting ~Beth Suter	111
Cautiously Masticating ~Jill Boyles	112
Chewing It Over ~Linda Hofke	113
Glass Jars in Root Cellars ~Barbara A. Meier	114
Clementine ~Susan Mahan	116
Apple or Orange ~M.J. Iuppa	117
Fallen Apple ~Larry Schug	118
Acknowledgments	121
Contributors	123
Index (by poet last name)	137
About The Poetry Box®	140
Order Form	141

Introduction

In Maslow's *Hierarchy of Needs* pyramid, we find food at its base, representing one of our most fundamental human needs for survival. But food not only nourishes our body, it can feed our spirit, nurture our very essence. From the moment we arrive in this world, whether suckling our mother's breast or feeding on a bottle, we learn that food equals comfort.

Some of our most memorable moments in life are shared with loved ones around the dining room table or cooking together in the kitchen. Celebratory feasts are a part of almost every culture whether it be for a holiday or to memorialize a significant accomplishment or occasion.

Take for example, Thanksgiving. Aside from the parades, football and Black Friday sales-mania, the main focus has always been a glorious meal served with a helping of immense gratitude. Often, it's the one time each year when we can visit with loved ones that perhaps live far away. And the preparation and anticipation may start several months in advance, as noted in the poignant poem, "The Seeds of Thanksgiving" by Tricia Knoll:

> *In May, I poke eleven pie pumpkin seeds into dirt.*
> *I bless them into a star shape ...*
> *... I wonder if I'll be here at harvest ...*

Food can also bridge the gap between generations. Something magical happens when a grandmother shares a sacred family recipe with her grandchild, teaching her the "old ways" of making a meal from "scratch." Bread never tasted so good as the piece sliced from a still oven-warm loaf, kneaded just hours ago by aging hands coupled with the smooth fingers of youth.

I have a blue tin box in my cupboard filled with recipes collected through the years. Some are clipped from faded newspapers, some are printed on the back of canned food labels and some are handwritten by my mother. My grandmother didn't like writing down her recipes. One of my greatest regrets is not paying more attention or taking notes when I watched her make her syrupy pear preserves — an old family favorite served over vanilla ice-cream or piping hot biscuits. I guess that's why I could so easily relate to the panic felt in Connie Post's poem, "Stock" as she:

> ... searches, she toils
> For the small hand written index card her grandmother gave her
> Thirty years ago ...
> ... Cannot recall the soft cursive lines at the beginning ...

Of course, "panic" may be a bit of an overstatement, considering I've been lucky enough in life to always have the means by which to feed my family. I can't really recall a day of my children going hungry, besides the occasional self-inflicted hunger due to finicky, picky eating. I am humbled by the fact that millions on this globe go hungry every day. I remember the stories of generations past when sugar was rationed and a simple birthday cake was a luxury during world war. And how menial labor and piece work was often the only means for a mother to put food in her child's belly, as Rachelle M. Parker reminds us in her poem, "Keeping Count"

> Fingers that push threaded needle ...
> Know 10 pockets gets you a pound of greens
> Know 50 pockets adds a chuck of meat ...

Today the world has yet to vanquish hunger on a global scale. And in the most prosperous places on Earth, we find growing populations of obese, yet malnourished citizens. My inbox is filled daily with requests for another signature to fight against conglomerates who favor sizeable profits over quality food, or as Laurel Feigenbaum so eloquently coined in her poem, "The Corruption of Gazpacho"

> ... better eating through chemistry.

I read articles quoting executives who claim water and good health are not a human right. And I can't help but wonder, when will this madness finally come to an end?

Perhaps we should all slow down our pace on the hamster wheel a notch, and return to the days of "an apple a day…" Maybe it's time to cook up some chicken soup to soothe our common cold instead of another antibiotic to compromise our immune system. Let's take some advice from Deborah Meltvedt in her poem "Cookie Dough (or What Didn't Make Us Sick)"

> …remember what it feels like to
> taste ourselves uncooked.
> Before heat and flame and medicine
> make everybody
> very, very sick.

It is with much gratitude and humility that we thank all of the poets who shared their stories, their heartbreak, their hope and their fondest memories as it relates to food. We invite our readers to share in this bountiful harvest of food for thought and to taste the wonder of these glorious poems.

~ Shawn Aveningo
October, 2015

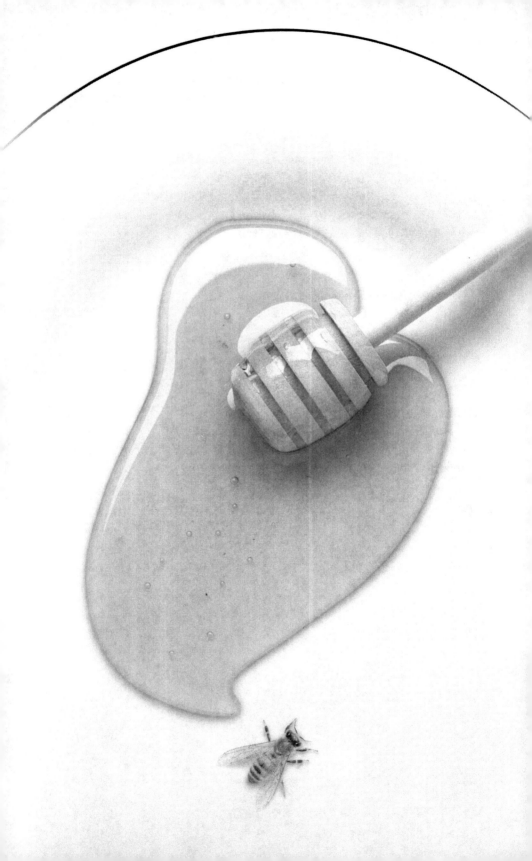

Paulann Petersen

Appetite

    Pale gold and crumbling with crust
    mottled dark, almost bronze,
    pieces of honeycomb lie on a plate.
    Flecked with the pale paper
    of hive, their hexagonal cells
    leak into the deepening pool
    of amber. On your lips,
    against palate, tooth and tongue,
    the viscous sugar squeezes
    from its chambers, sears sweetness
    into your throat until you chew
    pulp and wax from a blue city
    of bees. Between your teeth
    is the blown flower and the flower's
    seed. Passport pages stamped
    and turning. Death's officious hum.
    Both the candle and its anther
    of flame. Your own yellow hunger.
    Never say you can't take
    this world into your mouth.

Linda Ferguson

Let those love now*

I want to make you all some good, hot food,
to feed you polenta baked until it forms a crispy
peppered crust, then serve up ruffled greens
and soft biscuits filled with steaming fruit.
I want to cook all morning and afternoon,
to make you valentine-shaped cookies
sprinkled with cinnamon, and also pies
packed with dark red cherries that sing
with a deep, bubbling juice,
like a choir joining voices beneath
a domed ceiling. I want to feed you all,
from the grandmother left sitting alone
in a shadowed room to the cool, pale sister
with the cracked-plate smile.
Come, let's all take our places at a table
where our combined brilliance will outshine
all the candles and the stars and the sun at noon.
Let's pass our stories to one another
like a bowl of plump, green olives
or a basket of warm, sighing bread.
Here, at this table, we can all savor the alchemy
of a creamy cheddar cheese laced with chives,
and when we're done feasting, we can
each have a slice from a single cucumber,
so that its sweet, clean taste will linger
on our tongues.

*Thomas Parnell, Translation of "The Vigil of Venus," attributed to Tiberianus;
"Let those love now who never loved before;/Let those who always loved, now love the more."

Jan Duncan-O'Neal

The Trouble with Cooking: A Poem of Compulsion
  ~ *after Billy Collins*

The trouble with cooking, I thought
one chilly afternoon in January
as I was reading recipes — a mountain
of magazines avalanching to the floor —

The trouble with cooking is
that it compels me to cook up more exotic dinners,
more soup filling pots with fish bones and seaweed,
more ducks wild with rice and candied pecans
redolent of garlic and ginger.

And how can I ever stop?
until I lighten up with soufflé
sharing a small plate with green salad.
Sans rice. Nuts optional.

Then there will be nothing left to do
but quietly nibble raw carrots,
sit with my hands folded on my skinny hips.

Cooking absolutely consumes me,
makes my head dizzy like gulping four glasses
of champagne, then turning round 'n round
wobbly like a giddy little girl.

Cooking forces me to empty my herb shelf,
all the produce from my refrigerator,
and wait for Roman candles of creativity
to burst from my brain.

And after that comes the urge
to dream myself a television celebrity

composing poetry as I whip up meringue.

Oh what egotistical gastronomical snobs
we pretentious cooks are! Imagining
our true place, center stage
on The Food Network. Wearing
a chef's stove pipe hat, pulling out rabbits
and ragout under stage lights. Juggling
crepes. Chortling *Bon Appétit!*

The reincarnation of Julia Child who lured me
away from the comfort of Betty Crocker
to my newest obsession, French cooking.

Linda Flaherty Haltmaier

A Benediction

An eager supplicant strokes
the velvet rope, anxious,
muttering like a novice with her rosary,
foreign phrases that will
divulge her darkest secrets
to those in black
who dole out the healing balm.
Dispensers of a salve protected
behind walls of glass and gold.
She steps forward,
eyes raised in a half-question,
a riot of pastels arranged
in perfect rows before her,
desires tumble out —
chocolate, citron, framboise —
as nimble fingers slide
holy discs into boxes of mint green.
A nod dismisses her down the line
where she sleepwalks
through the tally,
tipsy from the perfumed air.
She steps into the Paris street,
fumbling with the seal,
she lifts the host in silent prayer,
and lets it land on her tongue.
A communion of chocolate
and acolyte,
bliss in one bite,
There is a god
and his name is Laduree.

Lori Loranger

The Cheesecake Response

This chaos of existence
the terrifying dreamfalling
that's all impending disaster
with no splatting clash to end it
no final impact
on the perpetually approaching ground

It makes me want to bake a cheesecake
with fresh mascarpone
and hand-crushed crumbs for the crust,
garnished with tart jewels of raspberries
just off the vine

Merely thinking of it calms me,
the precision
and order
Complete control in my own hands,
down to the last burgundy thimble I place on the top

I can survive the trip,
this journey of being —
the details of the final landing
don't matter.

I can center myself,
beating eggs to a lemony lustre.
I can stop time
in this instant of transformation
I am strong and able
and can respond
without panic or terror,
I can turn impending disaster
into perfect
      cheesecake.

A.J. Huffman

Because Throbbing

pain behind my eyes, strong enough
to fuzz my vision is not a good sign,
I know the stroke I will
eventually die from is afoot. It has been
sparked by my niece
who treats apple juice
like illicit spirits, diluting them:
one part 100% apple juice, three parts
water. I know apples are already something like
99% H2O, so she is really only granting her
6-month-old daughter exponentially < 1%
actual apple anything, and looks at me
like I have lost my mind when I explain
as such. In attempted escape

I jet off to *Green Tea*, the single
best Chinese take-out restaurant
on the east coast only to be greeted
with their new up-charge policy. As I
am one of those strange people who like
more steak than pepper in my Spicy
Steak 'n Pepper combo, I proceed to order
extra. The barely-12-year-old who takes
my order in broken English tries
to explain that extra is now charged
by the dollar. *How many dollar*
you want? I wrack the very basement
of my already bleeding brain for some
semblance of an answer, find nothing
but the question I retort: *How much extra*
steak do you get for each dollar? Seemed
logical to me. He says he doesn't know,
they don't measure. I run

for the nearest bakery counter, grab two
chocolate chip muffins and a dozen brownies
as I struggle to hold on to consciousness
and sanity. I know neither is possible. This must
be the end, it cannot get worse. I bite
into the gooey center of the first confection,
hear the blood cells start to regain their sense
of direction. The pressure takes
a breath. I just might make
it to tomorrow after all.

New Spring Rites

In life's autumnal waning,
I've forsaken prayer at the altar
of garden plot perfection:
broccoli aligned in the front row
like a synchronized marching band,
bushy snap beans splayed
along a furrowed spine,
prodigious zucchini assigned
its own corner abode,
red chili peppers interspersed
— in surveyor precision —
with sweet cherry tomatoes,
and just a few pumpkin plants
strewn along the distant border —
one of which will snake
a viney tentacle into
the unkempt woods beyond,
only to reappear
in August's incandescence
dangling a comically elongated,
orange-ribbed offspring
from a low-hanging limb

Yes, this year
I'm casting aside
sowing obsessiveness,
taking up, instead,
an unholy lust
for planting
row upon messy row
of Heath Bar Crunch
ice cream cones

Jan Haag

Pi/pie

Had they explained it to me in math class
using the circular plate, pressed in a crust
and prettily fluted the edges, added a filling

tempting to taste buds — apple, cherry,
any kind of berry, pumpkin — but not mince,
never mince — then baked it to a gentle bubble,

I might have understood or at least gotten
a glimmer of the miracle of mathematics.
But being told that pi is the ratio of a circle's

circumference to its diameter made no sense
to my teenage brain. It was all I could do
to remember its first five digits — 3.1415.

They held no meaning for me — I could not
taste, touch, feel those symbols. But pie, I
could understand — Grandma's cinnamon-y apple

with its lattice-top crust. A small Chinese man
walking through his restaurant with his
banana cream (a recipe, it was said, that he

brought with him from China).
A man I loved fork-feeding me bits
of cherry pie he'd made from scratch.

Pie, it turns out, is love in all its infinite forms.
Numerical or baked, it is a constant. It is both
irrational and transcendental, and, I have

learned, this miracle of numbers and dough

and filling continues, without repetition
or pattern — on and on and on, ad infinitum,

amen.

Nathan Tompkins

Sin Eating

Tonight, dine on sin seasoned huckleberry pie,
fresh whipped cream lust on top, melt into the hot wrath crust,
absorb past regrets, hurts into the blood, into the skin.

Raise my right hand to her cheek, catch
envy infused tears in a silver thimble, drink
mix with Purple Moon Shiraz, poured in an oak glass.

The fork slices through the flaked layers
of lightly burnt golden crust, North Idaho huckleberries
freshly picked with pride, lift a bite to the mouth, taste
the gluttony, chew, swallow, take another greedy bite.

Lick the remnants of pie from the plate, drink the last wine,
feel the sloth of the full stomach, toss the wooden dishes
into the fire to smoke, to burn away a lover's sins
baked into a huckleberry pie, taken for my own.

Linda Ferguson

The Surprise Inside the Cake

We were still a couple of kids,
all dressed up like adults —
his charcoal suit with tails,
my white dress with a lace-edged train —
we had Pachelbel playing on the church piano,
boutonnieres pinned to our brothers' lapels,
and bridesmaids holding bouquets
the same shade as their chiffon gowns.
The reception, though, was a different story —
a party in my parents' backyard,
with my high white heels a little stained
from sinking into the soft grass.
We had a keg of beer and some
trays of food set out on a picnic table,
plus a wedding cake with a surprise
inside that first slice. Instead of
the vanilla layers with the skim
of raspberry filling we'd ordered,
here was a silly, garish thing,
as if we'd pulled back a curtain and revealed
an out-of-town aunt with spangled fingers and a brash,
knowing laugh as big as her hat. Instead of a pale,
well-behaved pastry, this cake was flaming pink —
like the thick flamingo lipstick on a drag queen
about to step on stage or the mini-dress Barbie wore
the night she tore off for Malibu in her plastic car.
How to describe what we fed each other
with our fingers that day —
was it simply sugar and shortening or the gaudy
flavor of caramel corn and carnival rides
that its glaring hue implied? Or maybe our tongues
were touched with something else —
a hint of salt, and the essence of

a small borrowed boat setting out to sea;
maybe we opened our mouths and tasted
not the cake, but the white peaks of promise
folded into some weighty substance
we could not yet name.

Boutheina Boughnim Laarif

Cookie-lover

I think of you
When I bite into
My almond cookie …
I don't want to lose a crumb.
Though I let some
Fall on my breast as daisies …
Then brush them aside,
Letting them settle on the ground:

Crushed bounties …

Debra McQueen

I Never Wanted Dinner

All I ever wanted was you —
Like a piece of chocolate cheesecake
Or tiramisu — either dense
Cream or fluffy ladyfingers
Tickling down my midline to that
Sweet place you treat with raw hunger —
So rich — less often was plenty —
Then you had to go and leave her

Laurie Kolp

Food Calendar Souvenir

I see you fared well in New Orleans
while I stayed here with the kids
eating pepperoni pizza &
leftover pepperoni pizza.
Look at these delectable pictures,
how sweet of you to think of me.
Friday night did you dine on Trout Royale,
or perhaps Smoked Salmon Crostini?
We ate the usual Lenten fare —
tuna casserole and canned peas.
Mmm … the Lemon Crostata
looks divine, and it tops my birthday month.
I know how much you hate lemons, dear.
I bet you chose cheesecake instead.
Yes, yes, with strawberries.
Oh my god! I'm jealous — while you
breakfasted on these fresh beignets,
I popped frozen monkey bread
in the microwave.
I see you ate well in New Orleans
while I stayed here with the kids
feeding them everything they love.

Jane Burn

Eggs, Three

Cool in my palm, brown with a tattoo of numbers,
little bald heads, giant beans — I wish on them
for a beanstalk. A goose to lay me golden ones.

Tap, tap, crack. A chip of shell makes the shape of France
in the albumen sea — I fish it out, wear it like a hat
on my finger-tip. The dot of wasted embryo brings

utter sadness to the swell of yolk — in the middle of my cake,
a nothing baby unless I spoon the little death away, make
a funeral with kitchen roll and bin. Butter, creamed with a crisp

of sugar — fluffed to a wonderland of fatted mountains,
a flood of beaten, sticky rain, poured upon their tops. A sift
of snow, a powdered blessing, knocked by the heel of my hand

from its basket of sieve — it settles in virgin smooth and I fold
with steady pleasure. Trap the air. Cocoa in a bitter swish,
uncapped vanilla filling the room with calm, the gentle hum

of the oven makes a song for the afternoon. My son will remember,
I hope, the smell of his mother's cakes. Too many, more than we
could ever eat, when the mood to make them comes upon me.

Look! Look what I did for you! Rows of fairy-buns, domed with ice,
sprinkled with rainbows. Freshly turned out sponges gusting steam —
halved by knives, their pillowed centers weeping jam.

Elizabeth Moscoso

Majesty

Infused with the Californian summer
heat, the air is thick with the steady stream
of steam, spewing and sputtering
out of the boiling pot of black beans
on the stovetop, dark liquid spilling out
seeping and staining,
tortillas toasting into warped brown discs
in the old white toaster oven.
Sientate, sit.
Watch as she stirs the pot,
bracelets tinkling,
her hair pulled up high on her head,
thin curly wisps loose
and fallen,
the knobs of her spine
slightly visible on the back her neck.
Here, she reigns her kingdom
of dented pots and thick-bottomed skillets,
Queen of *arroz* and *frijoles volteados*,
The stalks of wilting green
scallions bow down to her …
all hail.
Watch as she rises
on her delicate tip-toes,
reaching for plate on a cabinet
on high,
Scooping beans and rice in neat little piles,
tortillas crisp and proud, placed
on the plate in front of her
husband who doesn't notice
the slightly bitter
after-taste: the essence of the her dead dreams,
her secret ingredient.

Judith Skillman

Lengua

They called it, after it was boiled
and skinned, the pink and gray moss
cut like a banner from the rest.

Because they — happy, healthy, ran to the plank —
a wooden table like the talking
dreams I had the night before,

I ate the pick-thin pieces
on my straw plate. Not too hot
nor cold, Mediterranean, room-

temperature. There's a certain conceit
in holding a fork so small. Once
the fingers touch the lips,

a bit of grace comes into the body.
Sometimes heavily seasoned.
Other times with mushrooms

and watercress picked just hours
earlier from the creek — like a salad
perched atop an island.

A woman is the same in another language,
and also a man with his knife.
This organ of many names,

a bit tough, harsh with the Polish horseradish,
I could say it never melted.
But that would be facile — for a complex

problem such as eating a cow's tongue
far more argument is required,
more discretion, a pinch of salt,

a salt lick or a lame horse,
and all the ways lies stick
like feathers to the back of the throat.

Paulann Petersen

An Atlas of Taste

First and quick, its tip darts to test
the world for sugar — oblivious to all else.
The tongue senses sweet,
and only sweet, at its apex.
Leaves the rest to those parts of itself
lagging behind.

Salt it detects on both flanks, an inch or so
to the rear. Sour it sidelines to the back
even farther, right and left.

Oh, easy enough a tongue can say
candied, briny, squinch.
But only across its thick base —
nearest that lout, the throat —
will the tongue recognize what's hardest
to swallow. There's plenty of time, too much
time to say what's bitter.

Tammy Robacker

A Reconciliation

When the tantes arrived oblivious
with their air kisses and teased hair,
I frisked their drunk husbands. Uncles

who wore their white bellies swollen
in tight shirts over leather belts like Stöllen
loaves. Lounging low in armchairs, they called

for my company. So I laughed at their jokes.
I coaxed them for treats. It was a restitution.
The gentleman's agreement. I dug pocket deep

to appease us each by reaching in
to pull out hard penny candies or
wrap my hand around a tangerine.

Heather Angier

Gobstopper

I watch his heart
    harden —
        each school day
  pushed up against the others,
layers so packed —
      it could break jaws.

If he hides it for later
    I'm afraid
        he'll forget
he put it on the bookshelf
between *Amulet* and *TinTin* —

or worse,
          that he'll find it
      stuffed in some pocket
all-covered in lint,
    and then accidentally
      drop it —
           brittle star
exploded on the blacktop.

If only I could carry his heart
    for him   safe
      in my animal-mouth
  licked and sucked
      like a bruise — each
tempered coating
    dissolved to the last
soft, chalky center —

sugar sugar, teeth aching.

Penelope Scambly Schott

Looking at Bread

1. Looking at a Torn-out Magazine Photo about which the Writer Knows Nothing at All

We are standing outside a commercial bakery
in a provincial town in Nigeria
The metal shed roof overhangs
the cement patio where women wedge
long loaves into blue plastic crates
The women will fan out
to neighborhood markets
with crates on top of their knotted head scarves
Under the bright knee-length printed tunics
flowered wrap skirts cling to their buttocks
The crowd of men in the shade of the shed roof
stand with their arms crossed
One man in an orange-striped shirt
stares without pretense
Beyond the edge of the torn-out magazine photo
drivers honk and a policeman in khaki shorts
with ribbons across both shoulders
stands on his raised cake stand
in the middle of the traffic circle
blowing and blowing his whistle
The morning grows warmer
I have never been to Nigeria

A slender girl in a plastic chair
lifts one hand to cover her mouth
I don't know if this is really Nigeria or not
I do know I am old and no longer cover my mouth
A young woman in a tight white sleeveless t-shirt
looks straight into the camera
The woman's breasts will not always be this high

2. Something about which the Writer Knows Too Much

Here's what I know about bread and the world: most men in most places assume that some woman will feed them — it might be a mother or a grandmother or a wife or a girlfriend or a sister or an eldest daughter — and if a man isn't home he can step into a bar and a girl will bring him a jerky stick or an egg soaked in beet juice or something fried on a griddle and he will never have to think about where the food comes from because it's in front of him like the air he breathes, a blessing with which he is by right endowed, even when the bread he eats may have been carried on the heads of women, their strong necks navigating the streets like swans cutting across a lake while the men in the café sit over coffee and watch how the women's buttocks move under cloth.

In most places the men have carts or bicycles or oxen or trucks or motorcycles or scooters to carry goods from place to place, or else they have women to do it. Nobody thinks this is strange. Maybe somewhere here in America a man is pushing a supermarket shopping cart. Maybe I am a three-year-old female child with my plump little-girl thighs wedged through the front slots of that shopping cart seat. Maybe I won't ever stop screaming.

Connie Post

Stock

She has never had soup made from the stock of a whole chicken
But she has spent her life adding the best ingredients

Chopping celery fresh from the garden
Uprooting carrots from the deep soil
Of a begrudging ground

She has hand rolled rich yellow egg noodles
To be simmered all afternoon
She has salted her aggression to taste
Unable to identify
What's missing,
What's wrong
What's missing

She has selected deep green bay leaves
That added only quiet disappointment
And sacrilegious steam to the dank kitchen air

The sage floats near the top
Like memories and bits of broken consciousness

She searches through her rich dewy gardens
And cupboards of impeccable spices, every day

She seeks ingredients
Like the good memories she can't find
From kindergarten on

She pursues the good soup
When she remembers being beaten
To the ground, to the ground,
To the forgotten ground.

She searches, she toils

For the small hand written index card her grandmother gave her
Thirty years ago
That told her she must start with good broth
It must come from the rich, moist bones of a whole chicken
Boiled for at least an hour or a lifetime

Secretly, she knows she lost card,
Cannot recall the soft cursive lines at the beginning

She cannot find her bones
Or herself in the flawed broth

Pieces of herself float to the top of the pot
And she stirs until the night goes still

Joanne S. Bodin

Chicken Matzo Ball Soup

pale thighs float in boiling water
moving slowly at first
then bouncing up and down
as bubbles of air pounce on
puckered skin
now beginning to soften

a sprig of parsley on top caresses
your thighs in seductive spirals
carrot-slices bob around you as if
to offer a jovial moment before you're — overtaken
skin begins to lose the tender luster
and you imagine you are on a beach
in the French Riviera
see yourself aging
sun-dried, too soon

but when the matzo balls are dropped into the mix
memories of your Russian grandmother
offer comfort while you tender up to the finish
her life in Russia was hard, but
even when they threw others into the pot
your grandmother knew the matzo balls
would always distinguish her from the others
reminding her of how she was meant to be a survivor
no matter how much they tried to neutralize her flavor

Georgette Howington

Scars, Philippine Sweet Potatoes and Mango

My five year old fingers pressed coconut oil onto the raised
red edge around the glassy skin, about the size of my palm,
on my Mother's brown thigh, not unlike a dozen or more other
scars on her legs painting stories like faded tattoos.
She pointed to one, "Bombers overhead, shrapnel pierced
my legs, my basket of sweet potatoes flying, flesh burning,
hot blood flowing but the only pain I felt was constant hunger."
For two years they ran from village to village; they hid.
During the day dressed as a boy she went to the old farm
fields and hands plunged into the womb of earth pulling
sweet potatoes to light, setting them free; a sacred find.
The assault passing over, she knelt to gather all she could
save, placing them back into the basket and running with the
others into a grove of mango where fruit laid next to rotting
bodies and she picked up as many as the basket would hold.
That night Tita Lola baked sweet potatoes in hot rocks, under
the tropical skies and the children ate the warm soft orange
flesh as if they were chocolate confections; mango juice
dribbling down their chins sucking on the big seeds.
My Mother stroked my hair as I rubbed the oil over her scars.

Jeanine Stevens

Sugarloaf

In fourth grade, the teacher was evil,
placed columns of math problems
on our desks, even before the bell rang.
By 9 A.M., I was defeated
and still three hours until lunch.

Anemic, no snack breaks,
by 11 A.M., weak,
then Geography, a photo
the lofty mountain in Brazil: *Pao de Acucar*.
Named for the refined sugar packed
in bread-like loaves,
it towered above Rio de Janeiro.
I could smell Sugarloaf baking,
crust cracking cinnamon,
coated in confectioner's sugar.

It held me until the walk home at noon
for leftovers, and a small helping
of pink watery Junket. If we had enough
dime size food tokens, (red = meat),
lunch was bologna on fluffy Wonder Bread
and bright cherry Kool Aid.

We returned to rest our heads on desks,
a symphony played over the loudspeaker.
Part of the afternoon, we knitted
squares for blankets, our soldiers freezing,
hungry in a distant European winter.

Paul Belz

Apple Strudel
~ *for Kate*

Brittle sweetness of cooked apples
cinnamon's tang, powdered sugar's quiet snap,
my teeth enter tender crust and I'm back
in Mother's kitchen. She gives me Lipton tea
with my strudel. I'm 9. She shows me Charleston steps,
laughs dancing through the tiled room. Dad grins,
distracted from the radio's news: Kennedy,
Russians, civil rights.

                              I want to linger,
but I return to this Italian-Austrian café
to share my delight with you.
Tan houses with brown sloping roofs
surround us, more sheep than cars,
and the Alps - breaker waves made from rock
yanked towards the sun, turned solid before they tumbled.
Snow crowned, they guide the coming thunder storm
our way. Folks in this café drink noon's wine,
coffee, feast on pastries. You taste my strudel,
hum "Edelweiss" as we did today
engulfed in crimson flowers and birds' flute songs.
The kitchen memory stays with me. I live twice.

Mariano Zaro

Plums

My father wraps plums with newspapers.
I cut the pages in half. He wraps the plums.
We are in the attic. It's summer.
We don't talk. He rolls the fruits,
his fingers twist both ends of the paper.

It's raining outside.

The plums look like wrapped candy.
He is meticulous, not too meticulous, just enough.
The plums have to be without nicks or cuts,
firm, not too ripe, unblemished.

The storms have been coming all afternoon.
That's why my father is home;
he couldn't go to the fields.

He ties the plums with a thin string,
like a necklace.
Five plums in each string, exactly five.
I don't know why.
His hands inspect the fruit, twist the paper,
tie the knots, do the math.
I hide my hands under the newspapers.
He is on a ladder now.
He hangs the strings from a wooden beam in the ceiling.

I pass the strings to him.
One by one.
Sometimes, unintentionally,
my hand brushes his hand.
He leans his body against the ladder,
rests for a moment, cleans his sweat.

My father is old.
The strings dangle from the ceiling.
Plums in-waiting like dull,
modest Christmas ornaments.

Fruit for the winter, he says.
As if you could wrap the summer with newspapers.
As if you could wrap your father's hands
for the future days of hunger.

Rachelle M. Parker

Keeping Count

    Berta's got a family to feed
    A husband, hands calloused

    A boy at her hip, a boy at her knee
    A girl resting on apron strings

    She come to know the meaning of piece work
    Hands that feel the fabric, heavy cotton or fine silk

    Fingers that push threaded needle for basting stitches
    Know how many pockets is needed

    Know 10 pockets gets you a pound of greens
    Know 50 pockets adds a chuck of meat

    And know 100 gets you a whole meal
    On Sunday, a chicken brought to a boil

    Flour, lard and water pulled together
    Rolled out thin, cut to squares, dumplin's

    Hot fatty stock, bubbles the dough to done
    Berta know 'bout keeping count

Christine Easterly

Echo

Her bare arms echoed her naked need.

Hungry, she pushed her tray down the line,
piled her plate with pasta and potatoes
stew and string beans —
all we had simmering on the stoves.

Drugged, she set down her tray
and laid her head to rest.
The meds made wakefulness hard
and the servers whispered
about her ungratefulness,
sleeping instead of eating.

He approached her,
laid a hand on her arm.
Rest, he said.
Your food will be here for you.
This tray
this seat
this moment of respite
is yours alone.

Sylvia Riojas Vaughn

Tomatl, Tenochtitlán, Before Cortés

In summer, yellow blossoms
yield fruit the color
of a warrior's blood.
My husband, Itztli, kisses
the crop's finest.
Little heart,
he whispers,
meeting my eyes.
My strength.
Today I think
of Itztli
warring.
Our hungry children
at play, I grind
fiery chilies
in a rough molcajete.
Eyes stinging,
I add what
he's blessed.
The red globes burst open,
bleed against the pestle.
Shutting out all
but him,
I take care not to spill
a drop.

Harvest Moon

In fields pregnant with pumpkins, we seven
women gather to hail the harvest, tossing seeds
and nuts like confetti, offerings for the titmice

and starlings, the catbirds and swallows
on their way down South. Bowls of muscadines
and gooseberries spill over for unpicky possums;

chunks of persimmon and pear tempt voles,
hares, and errant skunks. This ritual sharing,
a rebuke against winter's skeletal embrace,

reminds us to praise what is ever full: your grace,
the source of all holies, and soon, too, our bellies.
Under your maroon-gold gaze tonight,

there are apples to roast; ears of corn to pop;
pomegranate, quince, and huckleberry tarts to eat
by the hundredweight, when dance of thanks is done.

Tricia Knoll

The Seeds of Thanksgiving

In May, I poke eleven pie pumpkin seeds into dirt.
I bless them into a star shape in that limed bed, another year.

I wonder if I'll be here at harvest. I haul myself up,
grab onto a rusted scaffold for the vines to climb, drape
into the summer winds, mingle with wrens. Glad to be here
as their heart leaves sway into dry Augusts
and mildew in September.

Today four pies bake in my oven, scent of sugar, cinnamon,
ginger, cloves, a pad of crust. Winter's noon sunshine
pierces the clear vase of the last orange-blush rose above the sink,
graces my dappled pies cooling for delivery to our gathering —
four young children who, stuffed with yeasty rolls and raspberry jam,
will make room for whipped cream and pumpkin pie,
maybe only whipped cream.

On the front porch, four more pie pumpkins hunker
out of the freeze, thick of rind, slight
of seed, juicier than jack-o-lanterns.
For later, a second thanking,
glad to be here now.

Mary Kay Rummel

Vegetable Soul

> *"Your soul is a chosen landscape."*
> ~ Paul Verlaine

Or maybe the soul is a still life
like Cezanne's onions — crinkled skin,
astringent flesh, pungent breath
cushioned on a table like eggs in a nest.

They add depth to a stew without
becoming the thing like the blue wash
that's part of the undercoat
part of the shadow.

His onions dance, green fingers
all grab and clabber language,
green flames sing in the hearth
in the throat of the wine bottle
the molecules that make up my skin
the air between our lips.

Or maybe the soul is the inside
of a butternut squash that I split
with a crack of the blade
scoop seeds, oil flesh for the fire
in my hands, generations of hands
repeating these gestures
and the anxious pleasures of testing
for doneness and of the first bite that singes
the tongue and the voluptuous swallow.

Pallid offsprings of sun
warm winter bellies and glorify the bones.
Edible bodies with their miracle
of turning inside out.

Elizabeth Vrenios

Ode to a Purple Onion

O
odiferous orb,
purplish
ovular
O nettle's burr bite
O tubular tang
Of my sauce's just right light.
You who sweeten
the feast
are doused and housed
in the faint passing breath of
my guests and spouse.

O layered lump
that trumps my jejune tureen's bloom
pour more
and more
of your
petulant perfume
into my soup,
into my saucy galore.

O tasty Tranky Doo —
O natty Zumba you —
who heighten
my palatated
cheese-grated
top-rated stew.

O how you madden
and gladden
my hot pot's true spot
and cause

my tinning tongue
to sting,
and sing
a passacaglia
of your praises.

Susan Star Paddock

Massaged Kale Salad

Stay sensual, simple, close to earth.
Gather kale.
Discard beetles, caterpillars, egg nests and spiders.
Strip stems,
adding to compost.
At the sink overlooking the pond,
wash, spin and slice thin.
Squeeze lemon into extra virgin olive oil,
add pepper, honey, salt.
Massage dressing into kale
with oily hands,
feel the crisp dark leaves grow soft at your touch,
your skin grow soft in the doing.
Add color: red pepper, mango or tomato.
Toss,
In deep appreciation,
slowly,
eat.

Mark L. Levinson

Potato

> Pygmy skin of postal brown,
> flesh of dehydrated ice —
> meet me after the curdling heat;
> meet me after the oil jacuzzi;
> contact me after the cheese sirocco;
> steam to me after the bulb-extinguishing,
> body-Englishing,
> anguishless, languageless
> fire-footed
> wire-footed
> mash.

Joan Colby

Radish

Rose Red, Snow White duality,
it might have been a radish
that inspired such myths.

A perfect belly
of tartness, sharp, crisp, cool
and hot simultaneously
like an embarrassment,
a word spoken you can't take back
or the crazy love affair
you knew was going nowhere.

Turret of tang, peasant in a red cap,
not sweet not bitter
but purely itself, fast grower
shirking dirt from its Kremlin
pushing like a birth.

Smart as a slap,
nothing bloody about it,
brazen as a backside
jeering the salad from riddance
to uproar. Take this
red fist, white flesh
taste this
polka dancer, papoose, full purse.

Katy Brown

Diet

> "Death is not an end;
> it is a change in metabolism."
> From the *Book of Barely Imagined Beings*

Bend near —
    let me tell you a secret:
all life bleeds.

    crayfish
    chickens
    fawns
    grass

Science can hear the cry of distress
from a plucked fruit,
the sigh of trees when they thirst.

    All beings
    respire
    obtain and use energy
    respond to the environment
    grow
    reproduce

    Every living thing eats something else.
    It is the way.
    Hunger short-circuits reason.

That lovely, thin receptionist,
your gym-pounding boss,
a cousin who won't eat anything with eyes
— don't be fooled.

They consume life:
soybeans — torn from their stems;
brown rice — beaten from stalks,
a fainting lettuce.

It is the nature of life to feed.
The thinnest vegetarian will eat her enemies.
All life bleeds.

Suzanne Bruce

Sunday Brunch

At the restaurant
we request outdoor seating,

autumn winds wink as patches
of playful reds, yellows shout hello,

sashay past chatter and whiffs
of coffee and fried bacon.

We sit in the sunny Sunday warmth,
enjoy omelets stuffed with

cheese and tomatoes,
your smile wrapped

around my heart.
I savor the food and you.

Stepping out of my own delight,
I begin to notice

a family seated to my right,
mom, dad, young girl and boy,

each cocooned in their own minds,
no smiles, no eye contact,

how gray they seem
in the midst of spirited, splendid weather,

no noises except
the clinking of metal forks

scraping their eggs and hash brown
packed plates, feeding their mouths,

as if they were hoping
the food will actually fill them.

JenniferAnne Morrison

Luaus Are Coconut Scented Shams

True, I loved poi and haupia
but I more fondly recall
spending my childhood days
hiking to the volcano crater,
miles from crowded beaches,
or picking through sea glass shards
on shorelines covered in prickly lava flow,
too rough and black to draw many visitors.
My parents ritually
dragged my brother and I
to the weekend swap meet
where they'd buy us the whitest, softest
pork buns and chewy coconut mochi
filled with honeyed red bean paste.

Here on the mainland,
I suggest to my friends who honeymoon
on the islands that they seek out lave tubes,
twisting through the islands' red dirt,
and that they sample some spam wrapped in seaweed.
They always blink at me, then
mention the luau they're going to,
tell me about their hotel's amazing swimming pools.

Buffalo Wild Wings

I laugh at the timidity of the guy
in his black t-shirt,
blood-shot eyes
being rubbed by lazy fists.
The guy who eat chicken wings
with the mildest sauce
and plenty of napkins while
displaying his tribal ink armbands.
His shirt is too fearsome
to be taken seriously,
hollowed out skulls
and swaths of flame,
threatening chaos
while offering the simplest life epithets.
And his pants,
his pants are one step from plumber;
skinny jeans without intent.
But he's got one thing to brag about —
the coolest ride yet;
but only when mom is finished
with her iced tea
and chicken caesar salad.

Joan Leotta

Al Dente

We walked into
the new red, white and
green-themed bistro.
"Seat Yourself" a sign
by the register directed.
We did.
A smiling waitress wandered up
to our table as we studied
the chalkboard offering
of pasta-bilities
and other choices
artfully scribbled out
above the bar.
I smiled back and asked
"Is your pasta al dente?"
She sauntered back to the kitchen,
returning a few minutes
later. She reported,
"No Al Dente's ever worked here.
No one in the kitchen
has seen any sign of him."
We ordered pizza.

Al Dente: pasta cooked so that it has a slight hardness "to the tooth" when you bite a strand to determine if it is done.

Tricia Knoll

The Best Thing About Ketchup

is the odd bedfellows it makes,
Richard Nixon and I squirted cottage cheese

with thick sweet vinegar lush, how tomato sugar
waits to jump the bones of fried potatoes.

You can travel to Tibet
and still find ketchup in the kitchen.

With too many tomatoes, you can
cook ten pounds for one half pint.

Go ahead and hide flavors I hate
like succotash and corned beef hash.

Comparing Heinz and Hunts always works
to ease gaffes at a dinner table full of smirks.

That story about a sculptor, down on her luck,
mixing water and fast food packets — tomato-ade.

When you fork the runny yolk of a soft fried egg
mix it in, taunt kids with popping open eyeballs.

When you're ten, directing a backyard play,
you've got gallons of blood for foes you slay

while relishing the perfect red
of fire engines and the carpets of stars.

Taylor Graham

Avocado

At Customs, nothing is invisible.
Not the bottle of Herradura finest tequila,
nor the jockey shorts in your duffle.
Not the border itself, 30 meters from our feet —
2 gringos wishing to go back home,
standing beside our Toyota not moving.
Not the bludgeoning heat nor the vacant look
on a uniformed face as he explained
we could not take our avocado across the border.

Every crossing is a junction, a decision.
Relinquish that *aguacate*,
relic of a still-unfathomed world
we were leaving?
You turned the avocado in your hand,
lifted it as to a balance of justice;

with your other hand, pulled the pen-knife
from your pocket, sat down on the curb.
The uniform watched as you
carefully slit the fruit lengthwise and handed
me half. He watched us bite
into soft flesh. Cheeks smeared with just-
ripe forbidden green —
even with my eyes closed, I could see
him in the labyrinths of law, lost.

Linda Jackson Collins

Last Suppers*

Platters mounted on the museum wall
blue and white patterned like Dutch delft
imprinted with last meals of the condemned.
Prime rib and mashers says one.
On another, lobster and cobbed corn.
Muted insight into stomachs and souls,
a reminder that killers like ice cream too.
It could be easy to dismiss these hard cases —
brutal men unrepentant behind prison bars,
or so we picture them —
until a New York suffocation
or a snapped spine in Baltimore
tells us that too often,
guilt is gauged by skin tone.
I contemplate my own last meal wish:
peanut butter on toasted bread
salty chips and ice cold beer.
Simple fare to match simple wrongs
I think. But who's to say what favor
my fair complexion bought, and who's to know
how many crimes are meted out
as a consequence of our indifference.

* Inspired by Julie Green's Last Supper art project http://greenjulie.com/last-supper/

Andrew D. Viceroy

Grilled Cheese

Nothing will impress you: Baroda flatware,
tableside violins, a hot pink sunset ...
You escort gods and august mothers —
Oh the company you keep!

So no fancy rituals (and I won't fix up the place),
Just keep us warm Humble Skillet
and we'll stick together —
ripe cheese, golden bread, hot crunch!

Stephen McGuinness

Batch Loaves

That place
On the bread
Where it touched
Another loaf
As it rose
In the oven space
Is a scar.
Where one
Melded into one
And for a time
Became one
Supporting
Another as they
Rise together.
Only to be torn
Apart when
Fully formed
And perfect.

Dan Raphael

On Which Side My

kindness like butter. the kindness of butter.
the persistence of butter vs. water & soap. want butter on that?
bread & butter   bread & water   bread & soap.
to bleed butter. bred for butter content

the demands of bread: some violence but not too much,
some neglect, some heat — bread the balance point of several scales.
where flour and butter are merged to spread their web
sauce — melted in, blended with, disguising,
homogenizing.   from seed head to grain, winnowing in the wind,
abusing the husks, plaiting the stalks stacked above the ground
safe from those with more than 2 legs, crows
patrolling the borders

the smell of butter in hot macaroni, butterball, lardoons,
layers of buttered pastry elbowing for room with muscular steam
trapped in lungless alveoli, butter rising to the top,
curds and whey, cloudy slurry, white out,
snow cows here to rescue us, milk shakes, cheese coats

frozen butter for biscuits, room temp for roux,
as butter is to egg, as egg is to veal, bread volunteering
for the toaster bacon butter, garlic butter, clarified,
drawn, whipped; butter molds, butter mints, mona lisa butter

eddies of night butter as stars drip & melt.
nipple stars   stalac-teets, in the stomach looking out
to heal by congealing, revealing, molecules opening
their many arms to knit a net of chemical traffic, the same
skeleton, skin we've never seen
keeping some memory wells empty for what might happen,
the attic with extra beds, more hay bales than cows in the sky

Cassie Von Abst

Pickled Beats

Raise hell, or raise chickens:
mostly hens, as a personal contribution
to the destruction of the "boy's club".

Though I don't believe in the perpetuation of pecking orders
or national borders, unless they're the borders of my garden,
because blackberries will oppress the shit out of everything
unless you put up a trellis and
I don't know how I feel about trellises,
but this bush is taking like 99% of the resources so
if I could just provide it some upward mobility, maybe
lowlier plants can get some sunlight, too, and, holy shit,
do I believe in trickle-down theory?

Clearly not, no way,
not ever, not in my backyard, I discard the idea.
Like a done-brewed locally-roasted medium roast, it get's
composted, and I contemplate backyard plant unions:
I think cilantro has rights to sunlight, too
and before I knew it, I spent the rest of the afternoon
reconciling my love for cobbler with a blackberry's
tendency toward manifest destiny within my garden.

(But I think I have tincture for releasing the toxins of
these unforeseen homegrown moral dilemmas.)

"No edible vegetation without representation!"
I stitch the patch on my messenger bag as an expression
of solidarity for the snap pea liberation.

And the only cultural appropriation I can jive with
is sectioning off my fermented tea culture
into an appropriately-sized pickle jar to give to a friend.

And I pickle my beets and sprinkle them with sun-dried
heirloom sprigs of the words of the beatniks.

Asked a friend of a friend to sketch me a tat of Emma Goldman's face
to place on the back of my right leg 'cause Emma was a badass,
and when I hike up my pant, you can see I'm in it deep
with a rabble-rousing anarchist pushin' up against
these g-dang agrarian authoritarians:

These black-eyed susans always watching,
and Orwell is turning in his grave and I'm
churning butter on the front porch 'cause its a Brave
New World of DIY and I'm bent on creating the best
multi-grain buckwheat buttermilk pancakes for
spontaneous brunch with friends.

I take my eggs like I take my words:
free-range and roaming —
I'd sooner comb a homegrown vernacular:
ethically sourced, locally processed.

With natural-dyed yarn,
I could darn your socks or sew you a curtain,
and you be certain to give me a holler 'cause for, like,
85 cents on the dollar, I could cross-stitch a revision to your
division of labor, or hodge-podge the cracks in a class system.
I could macramé a revolution, papier-mâché a solution to the
degradation of community.

Because we
fight fascism with spicy radishes and folklore —
and reading Weber was always a bore, but
to toke up with de Tocqueville talkin' idealism in a nation
or the legalization of Mary Jane, and, if my name was Jane,
and I played the banjo in a band, we could call ourselves
Jane and the Rhubarb Jammers
and we could raise hell; we could

brew up a batch of outrage over access to education,
raise our voices, raise a garden bed, raise minimum wage
to reflect inflation; We could take action
when our heartbeats quicken,
man, we'd raise hell
and chickens.

Three Months After Her Funeral

The way sunlight fills our kitchen,
the sun itself far away, she, too, from where she rests,
beams through the glass, permeates this space.
Even now, she guides, her hands becoming mine
or mine, hers, as we wash parsley at the sink.
Together, we chop onions, garlic, greens.
Keep it simple, she is saying. Salt and pepper,
lemon on the salad. She is everywhere I look:
in the olives that we buy, Middle Eastern, cracked,
the kind she loved. In the feta from the Armenian store,
just right, not too salty. She's the *za'atar* spice — and sumac, too,
her cure for cold sores on the gums.
Our pots, the better ones, are gifts from her. Our glasses, too,
for drinking tea. She's in my envelope full of recipes,
hand-written as I watched her cook —
and in the phone call from my sister-in-law,
who craves her salmon. Tomatoes, cilantro, jalapeno.
The soups I make are hers: white bean, lentil.
As if she's watching what I do, I hear her praise
or scold — *not cumin, not in lentil soup* —
but I add a spoonful anyway. Testing, tasting,
I break some rules. Pasta on a Friday night.
I catch her scowl. It must be chicken, fish, or meat
for the Sabbath meal, not mac and cheese.
I soon return to chicken. But times are tough,
the business slow, and kosher meat's not cheap.
My husband doesn't hesitate:
We don't need kosher anymore, he says. *My mother's dead.*
He's right, I think — but then I see her cringe,
as when our daughter married out of faith.
It's up to you, she says, and turns to leave.
A woman builds, a woman destroys.

Jane Simpson

The Family Legacy

Emily Dickinson would have baked
this cake when she sent gifts to offer
neighbors the solace of food. Her words
were tied in ribbons in the bedroom.

The recipe comes dog-eared and greasy,
the words of women who made homes and cakes,
only the butter and eggs tempered
to fill mouths, block verbs that choke stories.

This cake serves as a peace offering for rage,
a trough for sweetness. It's batter to fill
the veins of women drained of bloods
they let for their children and husbands.

The women who make this cake cream butter
and sugar so light it's the softness they
touch — they use the tip of a little finger
to scoop a meager feeling onto the tongue.

The bakers beat their strain into eggs, pour
ease onto edges of bad days, then fold
in flour with a purpose that never
spills beyond their wilted aprons.

The women have an instinct for timing,
a nose that permeates hot ovens.
They know exactly when the cake is done,
lift up comfort and slice it into grandeur.

My Grandmother Was a Witch

Not an ordinary type of witch,
but a Stregheria who
listened to the heartbeat
of the earth,
the advice of the seasons.

In the planting season
and under a pizza pie of a moon
she buried fish heads in her garden
to conjure
the growth of herbs .

On Saturdays Ladies from the Avenue visited .
She listened to their woes,
and prescribed the remedy.

There was anise and basil
to drive away the evil eye,

catnip and clover
to captivate a lover,

mustard seed and oregano
to thwart a troublesome mother in law.

and thyme
to grow money.

Every Sunday a pot of red,
boiled and bubbled on the stove,
sauce made with secret herbs
and stirring.

I imagined her meatballs,
the testicles of cats,
that meowed their way
through the alley at night.

At night under the spell
of a glass of wine or two
She and my stogie smoking grandfather
would play Briscola.

Take that, and that, she said
as she slammed down
The King, The Queen,
The Ace of Spades.

Victorio Reyes

Bacalao
(An Excerpt from the Tales of Happiness Santiago)

Happiness
    was staring at the chickens,
        foraging under the tree,
navigating
            an   obstacle   course
of
        mangoes   strewn   across
            the   ground.

They reminded him of the pigeons
he loved to watch back home.

    "Ahhpeee, venga," a voice called from inside.

He made his way through the backdoor into the kitchen

    "Jue wanna try?"

His abuela pulled a piece of salted codfish from a small wooden case
and handed it to him; Happiness ate it quickly.

    "Es good no?" she asked rhetorically.

Big woman
    white hair,
        heavy laugh,
            light heart,
                walnut skin,
                    big hands.

He had only known her for a couple of days,
but his granma had already won him over.

He stared intently as she prepared dinner.

        Hot oil, aluminum pot, onions
           sizzle, hiss, pop
        bacalao, pilón, sweet peppers
          sizzle, hiss, pop
           recao, water, rice
                        simmer.

The aroma
    filled the room,
        filled the day with laughter,
            filled his cosmos with gravity.

Ann Howells

Banana Sandwich

Every noon that whole summer
Effie Mae settled her weedy butt
clad in white cotton underpants
on the lower step of the little ladder,
tucked her bare feet beneath
the upper step that served as a table.
She ate, without speaking, the sandwich,
buttered white bread and sliced banana
cut into four diagonal sections,
that Memaw placed there on a saucer
and drank a jelly glass of sweet tea.

Kimberly White

Peanuthead
~ For Caleb Westphalen

Why does a three-year-old shove a peanut up his nose?

Because the best way to really smell a peanut is to wrap your entire nose around it

Because nature abhors a vacuum and the empty space in the nostril cries out to be filled by the material mass of the peanut

Because at the age of three, the boundaries between body and peanut are not yet fully established

Because at the age of three, the concept of exploration has not grown far beyond the mysterious orifices of your own self

Because the injection path leads to the wall of the brain and even if you are too young to know it, the veil is thin between injection and penetration and this is where you learn your first lesson in recklessness

Because sometimes the wave of events takes on its own momentum, born from your inchoate intention to taste the peanut with your nose

Because at the age of three, it is still possible to taste with your nose, smell with your fingers, hear with your eyes, feel with your ears and see with your tongue

Because you put a finger in your mouth, you put a peanut in your mouth, you put a finger up your nose, why not ...?

Because it won't go up your teddy bear's nose

Because your Grandma won't let you put it up her nose

Because the measure of a man with a peanut in his hand is standardized by the value of the peanut itself, separate and apart from the value of the cargo in another man's hand and is therefore unequal in compare to the measure of the man with a peanut up his nose

Because recklessness can be addictive, and the moment you taste that first blood is the moment your mind turns from taste to addiction

Because at the age of three, the adrenaline of new experience is as common as blades of grass in the field, living in the very air in your baby-fresh lungs, prickling your nearly-new skin like ripening cactus fruit with every brand new breath

Because you're three. Because you can.

Deborah Meltvedt

Cookie Dough (or What Didn't Make Us Sick)

When I was a child I was told not to eat
cookie dough.
Do you want to die?
My mother's voice warning me of
rotten eggs and salmonella and other
killers I couldn't pronounce or believed in.
But I didn't listen.
The dough was better than the cooked bite.
Butter, brown sugar, Tollhouse chunks of chocolate.
I would eat half the batter.

And I never got sick.

Later, on college nights, when we
imbibed on what college girls imbibed on
it was the Pillsbury kind —
a log of refrigerator heaven,
sliced and baked in bars and cars
I didn't need homemade
We ate whole loaves, making us crave coffee
and cigarettes and more dough at 3 AM
We sliced and sucked and gobbled.

And we never got sick.

Years and years later, all grown up
and should know better, I still took the chance.
Swirled the sugar and the eggs and swallowed
uncooked love — even when my husband, not my mother,
warned me: *Stop! What about the eggs?!*
And I thought about it. I don't like eggs; not fried or hard boiled
or scrambled or towering on top of fancy French toast.
But I like them disguised — in vanilla and
cinnamon, settling into invisibility. Melting in America.

And I never got sick.

Years later, they stuck the dough in ice cream and coffee drinks.
But that wasn't the same.
I needed the sifting of flour; the rip
of the semi-sweet bag; the dance of the wooden spoon.
I needed the risk of devouring something on the edge
of being complete.

It should be this simple,
a recipe for cure:
IV drips of sugared dough
chocolate veins
floured cells
absorption of something that refuses to burn.

Because Radiation cooks everything — skin boils,
flesh melts, all cells stop multiplying.

We should remember what it feels like to
taste ourselves uncooked.
Before heat and flame and medicine
make everybody
very very sick.

Matt Hohner

When Living Well Isn't Enough, Invite Your Enemies to Dinner

Revenge is best served in a cold, crisp salad:
a bed of jimsonweed and wolfsbane leaves,
sprinkled sparingly with belladonna berries for beauty and taste
and sliced death cap mushrooms layered liberally for oomph.
Chopped bloodroot for a peppery zing;
castor beans for a fresh, ricin crunch.
Garnish with digitalis — so delicate, so pretty!
Eat with lead utensils; tidy up with napkins
made from poison ivy pulp.
Dress it in a light, creamy rattlesnake venomette.
Wash it down with a cool glass of hemlock tea.
For desert, mistletoe ice cream!
After dinner, relax, kick back, and smoke
a whole bushel of raw, unfiltered tobacco.

Sreemoyee Roy Chowdhury

Half-past Ennui

Let's stir up some trouble,
spiced with internal strife
seasoned with herbs;
mint, parsley, chives
grown in the backyard of the mind
at half-past ennui.

The world's torn apart in pockets,
on the printed side of the news.
You fold the world out
in neatly tucked in corners,
flicking its spine away from your heart
at arm's length from your humanity.

World politics makes my curries sharp,
briefly jolting you with their piquancy.
The beads of sweat glisten on your forehead,
Droplets of condensation twirl down the stem of the wine glass.
The perfect accompaniment to our fear of intimacy.

Let's rescue the world with our dinner-table chit-chat
Our intellectual debate on Palestine's raw screams
Iraq's barbarism, America's intervention
houseflies feeding on decaying flesh,
buzzing around mutilated screams of horror.

We smile at each other,
across the gentle wafts of detachment,
emanating from my soup of sun-dried tomatoes
lightly sprinkled with rosemary.

My grandmother told me stories of Naxalite Bengal;
a torn, dismembered city-state.
Fervent nationalism
Idealistic youth

Shotguns, shells, ineptly built explosives, police barbarism.
Woven with tales of risqué love.

Where's the time to render simple love complicated,
deep fry every emotion in a thick coating of unpalatable reason,
when just being alive is such a thrill?
Imminent danger and a throbbing sense of mortality,
love's zesty perpetuators.

Coconut oil, sandalwood and crushed betel leaves
summon her memories
on this sun-baked afternoon.
I taste the vanilla of tame privilege.
while the shrapnel of distant blasts filter through gently:
Some milk with your Americano, honey?
Unlimited butter, unlimited sugar,
our world has lost its flavour.

Ennui has claimed the heart and the soul,
apathy, the fad diet
suppressing the appetite for mayhem,
the desire for a revolution in one's heart
to love like no one ever has,
no one ever will.
to sip the warm broth of life,
slowly,
indulgently.

You break into the Crème Brule
with a satisfied snap of the crust
and then,
a deep plunge.
I hear the spoon grazing the sides of the little crystal bowl
The subtle flavour flirting with your palate,
teasing out a smile.

Let's stir up some trouble now,
spiced with the sweet and savoury
of living, loving and being.

Laurel Feigenbaum

The Corruption of Gazpacho

A sun-ripened sweet scented Early Girl
is violated by a syringe of liquid nitrogen
transforming seeds and substance into foam¾
where there might have been gazpacho.
Welcome to the world of molecular gastronomy.

Culinary corruption on the rise,
familiar food liquefied, solidified,
their molecules and atoms recombined
tease taste buds with new sensation..

Travel to Spain for foamed mushrooms.
England for snail porridge; edible paper in Chicago;
mango and Douglas-fir puree in New York.
Attend celebrity chef lectures on culinary physics.
Watch media demonstrations or order a home starter kit
available online, $69.99.

Make way Escoffier, Julia, Alice for kitchen-cum-chem lab.
Recipes in formula form, lab coats instead of aprons,
and pantry shelves stocked with chemicals
that read like supermarket labels on foods to avoid,
all bringing you *better eating through chemistry*.

Karla Linn Merrifield

The Grizzly Course

In Tokyo a bowl
of bear paw soup
is a pricey commodity.
Diners ladle out as much as
fourteen-hundred dollars
at posh restaurants
for the titillation of spooning
up those body parts
of *Ursus arctos horribilis*
swimming in oily broth.
Mm-mmm good,
the #1 American guest mutters,
swallowing a morsel of baby bear's
just-right right front toes,
earlier deboned tableside
for authenticity's sake.

An additional charge
is accrued if the patron
desires to keep the claws
as a souvenir of his Jap junket.
Otherwise, they will fetch
an equally tidy sum
at the apothecary
around the corner.

     ***

          It's a good year
for vandal kills in Alaska
& the harvest there
of bruin meat, pelts & teeth,
domo arigato.

Sarah Ghoshal

Foodie

It's just fuel, he says. Just something to keep you going through the drives and the periods of silence and the running running running and the questions and assumptions and insults. But I don't see fuel. I see the potential for hollandaise and charred ham, lime juice soaked ceviche with brown rice crackers, crockpot meals that simmer for hours during storms that look like the end of the world and all of its bags of potato chips. I see crisp white wine and oysters down the shore, a burger cooked so perfectly it's done the same way all the way through, Thai chili sauce soaked chickpeas served warm with German beer. I see conversation and an excuse to sit at a bar and watch baseball and you. Fuel is for cars. Food is my silent mistress, goading me from the pages of a diverse and interesting menu, laughing at my will to survive.

Carolyn Martin

Crock Pot Cooking in Terza Rima

The unhinged lid is dancing once again —
its measured steps a metronome for thyme,
potatoes, carrots, onions, free-range hen,

green peppers, garlic, waltzing in white wine.
Who said, *If you can read, you are a cook,*
was right — but only in three-quarters time.

They prophesy their meals will make me look
as skilled as Julia Child or Rachel Ray.
But what they do not spill within their books

are strategies when tragedies delay
the chopping up or cooling down. The call
that screams, *Your child upchucked three times today.*

The keys that laugh inside my trunk. The fall
that sends me to my knees before the gods
of saucery and gravy-splatted walls.

The *Flavor Bible's* geniuses will prod
my insecurity when I cannot
decipher formulas for blackened scrod

or callaloo or Philly pepper pot.
I am not intimate with tapenades
or okra. What is tripe? I prefer … *Stop!*

the timer chimes above *The Blue Danube,*
announcing the debut of chicken stew.

Claudia F. Savage

On the Guilt of Being a Well-Fed Poet

Late afternoon
some windy, snowy Saturday in February,
or unusually cold early May,
you will not be assaulted by cigarette smoke
or the thrum of coffee in the 8-hour pot
but by black-eyed peas gurgling a ham hock.
I wish I was one of those poets
who wrote by the light of the last candle,
who shivered in six sweaters, fingers blueing
at the tips, the electricity shut off
for nonpayment. I long for the gaunt-cheeked
look of desperate creativity, that gleam in the eye,
the hair wild and unwashed,
as if I'd recently climbed Everest,
forsaken the shower and used pages of Baudelaire
or Kafka for warmth between moldy, threadbare sheets.
If only Notley could sustain me.
The smell of cornbread in the cast-iron skillet
goes quite well with my beans.
I get up early to hover over
newly risen wheat-speckled dough.
Friends invited to dinner moan in pleasure
at my slow-simmered marinara. Sometimes,
I attempt a poem
before the dessert course,
but usually their hands are already reaching
for the pear-cranberry crisp, heads inside the freezer
for ice cream. The fruit's syrup stains their teeth a haunting pink.
Fattened, they leave my home silent,
and I'm left with the smell of onion
around each finger. I am thinking of the next menu,
perhaps butternut squash,
something to use up the last of the apples.

A sweet stew.
There is a chicken thigh left
and some grated ginger.
I am anxious to finish this poem,
banish pretense,
light the stove.

Jane Yolen

What the Muse Eats

Cold cuts, leftovers, things deleted.

Warm milk, comfort, a line well plumbed.

Percussive words, like pretzel, broccoli,
the snap of them driving daughters from the room.

Honey mead, sweet on the tongue,
fizzing in the brain, a rabbit hole drink
that changes yesterday into today.

The insightful verb, like crunch, like wallow
which — with a bit of wrist flick–becomes swallow.

The parenthesis, which licorice sticks
itself into a bend, encompassing opposites,
changing the mood.

And chocolate because everything
 — even poetry, even prose —
is better with that frisson of wonder,
the dark night that leaves you with
the need for just one more word.

Ann Privateer

Leftovers

vulcanize in the kitchen
layered centuries quicken

for a beer chaser to gush
with simplicity then splurge

over poor relatives who know
barely anything but meat

and a placid potato that
lurks next to the leeks

set on the counter for soup
out foxed to live another day

in accordance with strict dietary
rules of coherence that enter rules

of etiquette into a white wash
like graffiti wall where the recipe

focus becomes our next mystery.

Martie Odell-Ingebretsen

A Fly on the Wall Café

As I digested thoughts of mug warts and nasty nettles
from the plastic vinyl and the lace curtains,
I turned the pages of the menu
as if they were time itself
hinting at bologna omelets, liver and onions,
even chipped beef.

There was a hum inside that was bright
with sunflowers, and children
slurping long worms of spaghetti.
I even saw a glass of laughter milkshake
blowing a straw paper that hit my heart,
but I didn't see a single fly.

Would you like a glass of cool? the waitress winked
and made another line on her face.
There was precious room for another
so smiled was her skin
and lubricated by bacon grease and the cubed butter
slathered creamy yellow onto pumpernickel, raisin
or a sourdough slice of fresh backed every day bread.

Did I really settle for tuna fish and french fries, even a coke,
when I could have had a butter-battered blueberry delectable?
My senses were caught in the plates that passed,
breathing dumplings and real maple syrup.

I couldn't tell you what I ate,
but I know that I was full,
for when I returned home I found,
tucked into the neck of my best dress,
a napkin where I'd written these words.

In Ghent

where every Medieval street
holds a myriad of wonders

where the massive Castle of the Counts
still stands in the city center

where atop a belfry tower
a gilded dragon still guards the town

and the giant god Neptune
adorns the old fish market gate

I can only conjur up my breakfast
at the inn on Vlaanderenstraat

It's not the taste of smooth Belgian ale
in an outdoor café

nor the smell of butter cream truffles
in the corner chocolatier

but the beauty of a simple boiled egg
not too hard or runny soft

perfect in its white porcelain cup
alongside a fresh croissant

a plate of cheese and a carafe
of freshly brewed coffee

at the small square table
with its white starched cloth

napkin in my lap
in the tiny sunlit room

where we sat
my daughter and I

chatting about our day
in this place the gem of Flanders

Christine Kouwenhoven

I stopped by the side of the road

to buy a watermelon
bypassing the soft-cheeked peaches,
the lima beans like
river pebbles, smooth and shiny,
the corn for succotash.

I picked the roundest one
from the selection, scattered bowling balls
by the side of the wooden crates, and carried it
like a baby on my hip, gave my five bucks,
tumbled it into the passenger seat and drove home.

On the kitchen table, the melon
ruled the room, super moon full,
striated like the basketballs
that bounce incessantly in the cement court
just beyond the window.

It was difficult to resist its perfection.
My daughter caressed it,
feeling as I did when I carried it
the heat within — It's so warm! —
as if it contains summer itself.

Later I will slice it,
my knife running through the pink flesh
like it might through wet sand,
carving succulent squares
that I will chill in the fridge.

We will have them for dessert
each bite crisp and cool
as if we were diving into a pool
one last perfect time
before the season's end.

Oh Mango!

I long to take you hostage.
You blind me with yellow,
intense as the noonday sun,
seduce me with your nectar.

I am addicted.

You are savory and sweet,
without the cloying of peach,
the candy of pineapple,
the swagger of papaya,
or the timidity of plum.

Oh, Mango, you are your own fruit.

I can't get enough of you,
your good defenses will not deter
my passion. I slice carefully,
slowly, close to the bone,
scoop out all I can of your soft flesh
and suck your seed
until all your flavor is mine.

Oh Mango!

Dawn Orosco

How To Swallow a Butterfly

When you see it on the menu,
it is natural to be curious.
Do you really serve butterfly here?
Is what you want to say,
but when she returns
to take your order
you find your words
come out different.

Poised for enlightenment,
you tell her
you are curious about the butterfly dish,
but as she whisks away your menu
with only an
Of course you are
in response
her look of disdain
tells you so much more
than those four words.

Leaving no space for protest,
she abandons your table
deeming you
no longer fit to serve.

The dish comes too soon.
It arrives before you can explain
you were only hungry for
an explanation;
you did not want the butterfly
to die.

So you lift the spoon to your mouth

and try not to breathe —
ashamed
you now know
butterfly wings
taste just like
strawberries.

Shawn Aveningo

How To Eat a Strawberry

Pinch her leafy tuft between your thumb,
your index finger and middleman.

Watch the berry makes her approach,
your mouth juicing, laying out the Oscar carpet
for her arrival.

Bite — taking only half, at first.
Resist the urge to chew!

Instead,
let her red flesh pose, Rubenesque
atop your tongue.

Slowly raise your tongue like a drawbridge,
close it against your palate, collapse the space.

Taste her soft, sugary-tart explosion,
her power to evoke in equal parts nostalgia and fantasy

> — Dipping strawberries into a saucer of powdered sugar,
> swaying to *Dancing Queen* on the front porch swing.

> — Your lover finger-feeding you berries as he slithers
> up between your thighs.

Swallow.

Swirl & glide your tongue across your teeth, to catch
any wayward seeds, pretending all the while you're the star
of a 1977 Pearl Drops Toothpaste Commercial.

> *Mmmmmmmmmm.*

Reflect.   Repeat.

Differences

Bob hums over his peach
Bending his head close
To the dish
This sometimes fastidious man
Slurps to honor the juice,
Tongue chasing the drops
With religious relish.
"A good one?" I really didn't need
To ask. "MMMMMMMMMMMM,
An orange one," he answers
Knowing I prefer the white ones,
The less tasty but less messy,
The lesser altogether ones,
Because I have not yet found the grace
To give myself over totally
To a sphere of fruit.
But covertly, something in me warms
In watching his sloppy worship
His sticky persistent tongue
Probing, his teeth tearing
The last shred of pulp
From pit.

Claudia F. Savage

Learning Abandon

Once, orchards smelled like love ought to —
cinnamon and rot and leaves set to flame.
Sweet smoke. A day's obsession.
More blatant green. More red blush
across the cheeks. Perfect skin break
for our impossible teeth.
Tangy honey to coat the tongue,
to urge us on. To more.
Twelve a piece. More.
Ladder here. Higher.

And when the gold flush of an early sun
fell, I called to you.

No waste or excess.

You and me, reaching.

Jeannie E. Roberts

Oyster

You drop and slide
within silken tides
of eternity
slipping
between now and soon
swirling
through past and future
joining jelly fish
as it rises   then falls away

You could hold
the oldest pearl
the youngest seed
as you filter
then feed on plankton
but you've been caught

O how they crave
your mass of brine-softness
your primordial kiss   where
you clasp and clench
your jewel-prone chest
only   to be opened

O sea-swept *Bivalvia*
how you glow
on the half-shell
gleam
steeped in sauce   when
you're swallowed

You drop and slide
within silken tides

of eternity
slipping
between now and soon
swirling
through past and future
joining belly's dish
as it rises   then falls away

Cathy Cain

Cold Pizza for Breakfast

She rises and walks barefoot down the sunny road
through the grey-shingled village still sleeping,
out to the open sand and sapphire sea.

All perfect, meant to be.
She unwraps a briny breakfast,
savory slices of a salty scene —

bright tomato starfish, Kalamata olive snails,
onion urchins and garlic clove bivalves,
mussel-colored eggplant with its soft inner clinging.

Water waves in cheesy, mushroomy, roiled-sand muck,
and red pepper kelp — not too sweet —
just as she wishes the coming day.

She approaches the ocean's cold shock,
her hand touching rough, barnacled rock.

Mushroom Hunting
   ~ *for my grandmother*

>In the moment between
>winter and summer dark
>
>we follow the scent
>of oak tannin and cave
>
>where just-thawed forest floor
>hides meaty, buttery bulbs:
>
>the same brown-buff
>as the sun-dappled loam,
>
>as if the leaves themselves
>became morels.
>
>Beneath the swell and bulge
>of the hollows, they burrow up
>
>into a cold, sheer light,
>filling us with a wild infusion —
>
>the marrow of the woods.

Jill Boyles

Cautiously Masticating

unpitted figs,
sweet meat pressing
the tender part
of mouth's roof

pain nudged
out of infancy by ripeness
nurtured from winding, husky

branches stretched
to swallow the full sun.
Nothing can grow under these arms.

I imagine myself harvesting figs,
and I think of you.

Linda Hofke

Chewing It Over

Salt water taffy. That salty-sweetness
that as you pull its ends gradually thins

until it gently rips apart is not us. We split
in two with a snap, like sticks of spaghetti

being halved by hands then thrown into a pot
of boiling water. First argument our last.

Today, like umpteen days since, the world
confronted me with memories of you

as that *Sound of Sunshine* song you love
played on the car radio as I waited in traffic.

I wondered where you were at that moment,
what you might be doing. I contemplated how

I truly feel about you after all this time has passed,
pondered words I'd speak if you stood in front of me,

debated if you'd ever change your mind and soften
like noodles do when they've cooked long enough.

Barbara A Meier

Glass Jars In Root Cellars

What good is it to open jars
long-sealed on cellar shelves?
Rimmed in dust,
and encrusted in spider eggs?

If I took them off the cellar shelf-

(shuddering at the wispy touch of mummy silk)

would light reveal preserves or rot?

Could I hear the hallow sound
if I pinged the lid with my knuckle?

Would the dull thud reveal sooty strings of decay?

A seal broken by the years?

a stench of you long gone in the ground …

Or could I hold it to a light,
swinging on the end of a chain,
where the memories would be rich ruby red.

I'd climb the planks
of stairs,
feel the breath of cellar rock
at the nape of my neck.

I'd stride to the light,
and hold the memories high.

Maybe then to examine for cracks,

leaks of air, bulging sides.
Sniff for foul.

Would the memories hold with examination?
Or would the first touch of air dust the insides?

Just as I am sure your body now resides in dust ...

I take the church key,
apply with surgical precision,
pry the lid back,
and wait ...

Whiffs of crème de mint, Tanqueray, Oreos,
flypaper spit, and cigarette smoke,
on a late night prairie train ...
with the Perseids
showering us in August,
melting across a Kansas sky.

Then they are extinguished ...

burnt up ...

Like we are long since dead,
you in your coffin,
and I in my glass jar memories ...

Susan Mahan

Clementine

I easily peel the skin,
discovering the delicate sections
of the small seedless wonder.

My husband had been the citrus expert.
He made fruit salad and
methodically removed
every last shred of white pulp,
carefully extracting seeds
from temples and ruby reds
before offering me a wedge or two
as I flipped pancakes or turned omelets.

I sample a solitary slice,
savoring the juice of the Clementine,
but missing his steady lead.

M.J. Iuppa

Apple or Orange

In the wicker basket on the harvest table, an apple
and an orange lie obliquely, skin to skin
in the midday shadow. This sight appeals

to my hunger, yet I'm uncertain of what I want:
The apple is Empire–shiny red with flecks
of yellow, shadow of blue.

                    The orange is Navel —
plump and dimpled — a pleasure that opens
like a good laugh when I break its skin.

Today, the sky is grey and threatening snow,
but no snow comes?
No wonder I'm stuck here alone.

I close my eyes and pick the orange.
It has good weight in my hand,
and doesn't resist my thumb to its side.

Orange is instantly everywhere —
And out of nowhere, you, *dear child,* appear —
your mouth watering for half of the whole —

We both eat quietly
        side by side.

Larry Schug

Fallen Apple

I lift you from the ground
after a long fall
and a hard landing,
find you still quite lovely
as I shine you on my flannel shirt;
delicious as I nibble gently
around your bruises,
delighted, that at your core
I find the seeds of a new beginning.

Acknowledgments

We gratefully acknowledge the following publications in which these poems first appeared:

"Appetite" by Paulann Petersen was published in *Poetry* (Vol. CLXXVIII, No. 4, Modern Poetry Association) *and also The Wild Awake* (Confluence Press, 2002)

"Lengua" by Judith Skillman appears in her book *Angles of Separation* (Glass Lyre Press, 2014)

"An Atlas of Taste" by Paulann Petersen was published previously in *Understory* (Lost Horse Press, 2013)

"Stock" by Connie Post was previously published in *Danville Cultural Arts Alliance Anthology* (2006)

"Sugarloaf" by Jeanine Stevens was previously published in *Ophidian* (2010)

"Plums" by Mariano Zaro has appeared in *Tupelo Quarterly* (online) and *Diálogo* (DePaul University - Center for the Latino Studies, Vol 18, No. 1, Spring 2015)

"Vegetable Soul" by Mary Kay Rummel appeared in *Nimrod: 35 – Hunger and Thirst*

"Radish" by Joan Colby first appeared in *Albatross*

"The Corruption of Gazpacho" by Laurel Feigenbaum appeared in her self-published collection of poems, *The Daily Absurd* (Ficusfig, 2014)

"Crock Pot Cooking in Terza Rima" by Carolyn Martin appeared in *Allegro* (July, 2015)

"Mushroom Hunting" by Beth Suter was published in *POETRY NOW* (Summer 2015)

"Cautiously Masticating" by Jill Boyles first appeared in *Focus on Dalian's Newsletter* (2012)

"Clementine" by Susan Mahan was previously published in *South Boston Literary Gazette* (Volume 4, February 1999) and self-published in her chapbook, *In The Wilderness of Grief* (2002)

"Apple or Orange" by M.J. Iuppa first appeared in *The Comstock Review*, and was included in her first full-length collection, *Night Traveler* (Foothills Publishing, 2003)

Contributors

A.J. Huffman has published eleven solo chapbooks and one joint chapbook. Her new poetry collection, *Another Blood Jet*, is now available from Eldritch Press. She is a multiple Pushcart Prize nominee, and has published over 2200 poems in various journals, including *Labletter*, *The James Dickey Review*, *Bone Orchard*, *EgoPHobia* and *Kritya*. She is the founding editor of Kind of a Hurricane Press. <www.kindofahurricanepress.com>

Andrew David Viceroy has a fetish for urgent delivery: he's a writer, musician, and student of poetry and emergency telecommunications in Portland, OR. His poetry has been published in *The American Poetry Anthology*, *NW Creative Arts Magazine*, and artist Thomas Campbell's *Joke Fanzine*. His philosophy/psychology hybrid, "The Right Track and the Track That's Left: Exploring Predispositionalism" is available on Scribd. <www.scribd.com/AndrewDViceroy>

Ann Howells' work appears in *Crannog*, *Little Patuxent Review*, and *Spillway*, among others. She has edited *Illya's Honey* for fifteen years, recently taking it digital (and adding a co-editor, Melanie Pruit.) Ann's chapbooks are: *Black Crow in Flight* (Main Street Rag, 2007) & *The Rosebud Diaries* (Willet, 2012). *White Star, Blue Fields* (a book of her poetry paired with art by J. Darrell Kirkley) is forthcoming. She has four Pushcart nominations. <www.IllyasHoney.com>

Ann Privateer was born in Cleveland, Ohio. Los Angeles, California stole her heart. She moved there, completed college, married and moved north to raise a family. Ann retired from teaching and spends some of the year in Paris, France with family. Her poems have appeared in *Manzanita*, *Poetry Now*, *Tapestries*, *Entering*, and *Tiger Eyes* to name a few. Photography and painting are recent interests.

Barbara A. Meier is a kindergarten teacher in Gold Beach, Oregon. When she is not trying to survive in the wasteland we call education, she writes poetry to soothe her soul. She has been published in *A Quiet Courage*, *Miller's Pond*, *River Journal*, and *Poetry Pacific*. <basicallybarb@gmail.com>

Beth Suter lives in Davis, California with her husband and son. She studied Environmental Science at U.C. Davis and has worked as a naturalist and teacher. She is also an award-winning poet, a Pushcart Prize nominee, with pieces in *Tule Review*, *The Avocet*, *Literary Mama*, and *Albatross* among others.

Mrs. **Boutheina Boughnim Laarif** has obtained a DEA diploma (literature), Faculty of Arts, La Manouba. She is undertaking a PhD focusing on a postmodern approach to W. H. Auden's poetry and metrical art. She is a Lecturer of English literature. She has published articles which focus on philosophical, aesthetic theories of poetic rhythm, Nietzsche's theory of the lyric, and Heidegger's philosophy of art and politics. She also has several poems published in *Dytenium Journal*.

Carolyn Martin is blissfully retired in Clackamas, OR, where she has adopted a Spanish proverb as her daily mantra: "It is beautiful to do nothing, then rest afterwards." She does a lot of resting between gardening and writing. Her second poetry collection, *The Way a Woman Knows*, was published in February 2015 by The Poetry Box®. <portlandpoet@gmail.com>

Cassie Von Alst is a writer, biker, and barista in Portland. She co-organizes the spoken word group NoPoSpoWo and frequents a host of other writing/slam/storytelling events about town. Her work can be found written in fine ink on the back of the bar bill.

Cathy Cain is a writer, painter, and printmaker living in Oregon. She has enjoyed being a part of Portland's writing community, including Mountain Writers, the Attic Institute, and VoiceCatcher. Her first published poem appeared in *VoiceCatcher*, Winter 2014.

Christine Easterly is a Sacramento poet who follows the Amherst Writers & Artists style, leads a writing group and has been published in *Soul of the Narrator* and *Sacramento Voices*. She swims with a masters team in Davis and can often be found haunting her local library.

Christine Kouwenhoven is a writer/artist residing in Baltimore, Maryland. She is the mother of three with her husband, Nick. Christine has a B.A. in English/Writing from Connecticut College and an M.A. from The Writing Seminars at Johns Hopkins University. She works at Baltimore School for the Arts, where she is Director of Communications & Grants and helps to raise money for aspiring young artists: dancers, musicians, visual artists, actors, and perhaps some future writers too.

Claudia F. Savage once cooked for people recovering from illness and wrote *The Last One Eaten: A Maligned Vegetable's History*. She's had work in *The Denver Quarterly*, *Iron Horse Review*, *Nimrod*, and *Bookslut*. She teaches at The Attic and

Savage Poetics, is part of the poetry/music duo, *Thick in the Throat, Honey*, co-founded the late-night supper club Trash My Kitchen, and has been awarded grants and residencies at Ucross, the Atlantic Center for the Arts, and RACC. <www.claudiafsavage.com>

Connie Post is the Poet Laureate Emerita of Livermore. (2005 to 2009) Her work has appeared in *Calyx, Spoon River Poetry Review, Crab Creek Review, Slipstream, The Big Muddy, Valparaiso Poetry Review*. She won the 2009 Caesura Poetry Award. Her first full length book *Floodwater* was released by Glass Lyre Press in 2014 and won the Lyrebird Award. She enjoys reading and writing food poems as it sustains us, as does poetry.

Dan Raphael spent March in residence in south central Oregon, on Summer Lake, which fed him in several ways. Current poems appear in *Caliban, Make it True, Indefinite Space, Big Bridge*, and *Unlikely Stories*. His newest book, *Everyone in This Movie Gets Paid*, is aloft in search of a publisher. <Raphael@aracnet.com>

Dawn Orosco is a 3rd grade teacher whose love affair with creative writing began in elementary school. She spent many mornings of her childhood plugging away on an old electric typewriter while she chomped on Grape Nuts at the breakfast table. She has traded the typewriter for a MacBook Pro, but still finds she does her best writing when she is working against a deadline. <dawnoro@mac.com>

Debra McQueen is a special education teacher by day and a motorcycle riding poet by night. Her poetry has appeared or is forthcoming in *Red Triangle, The Lake, The Legendary, Undertow Tanka Review, Neon, WORK*, and *RoguePoetry Annual Review*.

Deborah Meltvedt is a high school teacher who loves to combine health and medical topics with creative writing. Deborah also works with Sacramento's 916Ink literacy project to help her students become published authors. She has been published in Sacramento's *Tule Review, The American River Literary Review*, and the true story anthology *Under the Gum Tree*. She lives in Sacramento with her husband, Rick, who is the true cook in the family, and their cat, Anchovy Jack, who is allergic to seafood.

A recent graduate from Marylhurst University, **Elizabeth Moscoso** is looking forward to focusing on her creative writing projects and exploring ways to combine her love of cooking, traveling and writing. She is a fan of reading, sunny days, bananas, Disneyland, and impromptu photo sessions. She lives with her family and three spoiled pups in a suburb of Portland. Her work has appeared on *Hellogiggles* and *Voicecatcher*. <elizabeth.moscoso459@marylhurst.edu>

Elizabeth Vrenios' poetry has been featured in an online poetry column: *Clementine*, and in a forthcoming anthology by Silver Birch Press She is a student of Judith Harris, Hailey Leithauser, Sue Ellen Thompson, and Gloria Boyer. She is a Professor Emerita from American University, and has spent most of her life performing as a singing artist across Europe and the United States.

Georgette Howington is a naturalist, horticulturist, gardener and writer whose niche is Backyard Habitat and secondary-cavity nesters. She is a County Coordinator and Assistant State Program Director for the California Bluebird Recovery Program. Georgette has had articles on gardening and conservation subjects published and most recently, poetry.

Since earning an MFA in English and Creative Writing from Mills College, **Heather Angier**'s poetry has appeared in many journals, including *ZYZZYVA*, which she always mentions because they paid her 50 bucks. Her chapbook, *Crooked*, was recently published by Dancing Girl Press. Heather lives in Oakland, California. <hangier@sbcglobal.net>

Helen Kerner was first published in the *National High School Poetry Anthology* many years ago. She worked in the corporate world, but never stopped writing poetry. Helen has been published in several Marin Poetry Center anthologies, as well as in *Stories With Grace*, and *VoiceCatcher*. In 2007 she published *The Journey*, a poetry and prose book about her 1993 bone marrow transplant for leukemia.

Irene Bloom is an emerging poet from Seattle, Washington whose work is inspired by her world travels, love of language, and sharing the written word with others. Her poems have appeared in *Poetry Super Highway, Drash Northwest Mosaic, Voices Israel*, and *Poeming Pigeons*. She also loves to prepare, share, and enjoy all kinds of FOOD with friends and family wherever she finds herself. <bloomwrite@gmail.com>

A Pushcart nominee, **Jan Duncan-O'Neal** upon retiring from a fascinating career in librarianship has settled in Overland Park, KS with her witty and loving husband, Bill. She enjoys editing the *I-70 Review* with three other poets. Her poems have been published in various journals including *The MidAmerican Poetry*

Review, Coal City Review, and Thorny Locust. The Lives You Touch Publications published her chapbook Voices: Lost and Found in 2011. Jan loves cooking, eating, and visiting art museums. <jando@kc.rr.com>

Jan Haag, by her own admission, is not much of a cook, though she makes her grandma's brownies at the end of every semester for her writing students at Sacramento City College. She is the author of Companion Spirit (Amherst Writers & Artists Press) and is working on two novels, as well as a history of Sacramento City College, which celebrates its 100th anniversary in 2016.

Jane Burn is a writer and artist based in the North East of England. Her poems have appeared in numerous magazines and anthologies and was long-listed for the Canterbury Poet of the Year Award, the National Poetry Competition and was commended in the Yorkmix 2014. Her work has been featured in two Emma Press anthologies and four Kind of a Hurricane Press Anthologies. She also had a single poem nominated for the Forward Prize.

Jane Simpson lives in Atlanta, Georgia, and writes for the nonprofit sector. She has had poems published in national and international journals that include the following: Ariadne's Thread, Main Street Rag, The Chattahoochee Review, POEM, and Poet Lore (with Honorable Mention, Ratner-Ferber-Poet Lore Prize). She can prepare a perfect pound cake for the oven in 16 minutes.

Jane Yolen, called "the Hans Christian Andersen of America" (Newsweek) is the author of over 350 books. Her work has won an assortment of awards--two Nebulas, a Caldecott, two Christopher Medals, nomination for the National Book Award, three nominations for the Pushcart Prize. She's the only writer to win the New England Public Radio Arts and Humanities Award in 2014 since its inception. Six colleges and universities have given her honorary doctorates. One of her awards set her good coat on fire. <janeyolen.com>

JC Reilly is the author of La Petite Mort and 25% co-author of an anthology of occasional verse, On Occasion: Four Poets, One Year. She lives in Atlanta with her cats and her husband, and was into baking fancy cupcakes long before it became a fad. She (sometimes) blogs about writing and other random things. <jcreilly.wordpress.com>

Jeanine Stevens was raised in Indiana (Corn and Bible Belts) and now lives in Sacramento and Lake Tahoe. Poetic influences include woodlands, inner cities, sacred wells and rivers. Besides writing, she enjoys Romanian folk dance, Tai Chi and collage. Her latest chapbook is, *Needle in the Sea* (Tiger's Eye Press). She is a member of the Squaw Valley Community of Writers. <stevensaj@yahoo.com>

Jeannie E. Roberts lives in an inspiring rural setting near Chippewa Falls, Wisconsin. Her second book of poetry, *Beyond Bulrush*, a full-length collection, is forthcoming from Lit Fest Press in 2015. She is also the author of *Nature of it All*, a poetry chapbook (Finishing Line Press, 2013), and the author and illustrator of *Let's Make Faces!*, a children's book. She draws, paints, and often photographs her natural surroundings. <www.jrcreative.biz>

JenniferAnne Morrison is a writer and ski bum turned elementary school teacher. Her previous publications include a poem in the July/August issue of *Cicada* and a historical essay in the Winter 2014 issue of *La Peninsula*. <jenniferanne.morrison12@gmail.com>

Jill Boyles' work has appeared in *Toasted Cheese*, *The Ilanot Review*, and *Calliope Magazine*, among other publications. She holds an MFA in Writing from Hamline University. She was the recipient of a Minnesota State Arts Board grant and a finalist for the Jerome Grant. In Turkey, she learned to appreciate the naked fig unadorned without the cookie coat. <jillboyles.com>

Joan Colby has published 16 books and chapbooks, the most recent of which include *The Wingback Chair* (FutureCycle Press), *Ah Clio* (Kattywompus Press) and *Pro Forma* (Foothills Publishing). Her work has appeared in journals such as *Poetry*, *Atlanta Review*, *South Dakota Review* and others. <joancolby.com>

Joan Leotta has been playing with words through writing and performing since childhood. Joan recently completed a month as a *Tupelo Press'* 30/30 poet and has work in *Poeming Pigeons*, *Knox Literary Magazine*, and *Eastern Iowa Review*. In addition to work as journalist, short story writer, author, poet and essayist, Joan performs folklore and "women-in history" stage shows. She often walks the beach in Calabash, NC with husband Joe where she collects seashells, pressed pennies and memories. <www.joanleotta.wordpress.com>

Joanne S. Bodin Ph.D., is an award-winning author, poet, and retired educator. Her book of poetry, *Piggybacked*, was a finalist in the New Mexico Book Awards. Her novel, *Walking Fish*, won the New Mexico Book Awards and the International Book Awards in gay/lesbian fiction. Her poetry has appeared in various poetry anthologies including; *La Llorona Poetry Anthology*, *Malpais Review* Vol.5, *The Yes Book*, *Glitterwolf Magazine*, and *Adobe Walls 5*. She plays jazz piano and is a watercolor painter. <www.walkingfishnovel.com>

Judith Skillman's new book is *House of Burnt Offerings* from Pleasure Boat Studio. The author of fifteen collections of poetry, her work has appeared in *Tampa Review, Prairie Schooner, FIELD, The Iowa Review,* and others. Awards include grants from the Academy of American Poets and Washington State Arts Commission. Skillman taught in the field of humanities for twenty-five years, and has collaboratively translated poems from Italian, Portuguese, and French. Currently she works on manuscript review. <www.judithskillman.com>

A nine-time Pushcart-Prize nominee and National Park Artist-in-Residence, **Karla Linn Merrifield** has had over 500 poems appear in dozens of journals and anthologies. She has eleven books to her credit, the newest of which *Bunchberries, More Poems of Canada*, a sequel to. *Godwit: Poems of Canada* (FootHills), which received the Eiseman Award for Poetry. She is assistant editor and poetry book reviewer for *The Centrifugal Eye*. Visit her blog, Vagabond Poet, where, among other things, you'll find out she is not Canadian. <http://karlalinn.blogspot.com>

Katy Brown is a poet and photographer whose work appears online and in several journals and anthologies, as well as in sundry formats. She has written, among other things, a multiple ending book, a series of short mysteries, and automobile humor. Her poetry has been nominated for the Pushcart Prize. As to food, she will eat anything. A neighbor once observed that she was the last of the great omnivores. <kbrown4081@aol.com>

Kimberly White's poetry has appeared in numerous journals and anthologies. She is the author of four chapbooks, *Penelope, A Reachable Tibet, The Daily Diaries of Death,* and *Letters To A Dead Man*; two novels: *Bandy's Restola*, and *Hotel Tarantula*. Find poetry and collage art on her website, as well as on Facebook and her boyfriend's refrigerator. <purplecouchworks.com>

Larry Schug is retired after a life of various kinds of physical labor, including recycler, groundskeeper, forest fire fighter, grave digger, farm worker and others. He is the author of seven books of poems, the latest being *At Gloaming* with North Star Press. He lives with his wife, dog, and three cats near a large tamarack bog in central Minnesota. <www.larryschugpoet.com>

Laurel Feigenbaum lives in Corte Madera, Ca. with her husband of 65 years. At 80 she gathered late-life courage and began writing. Her work appears in recent issues of *Nimrod*, *Spillway*, and an upcoming 2016 *Les Femmes Folles* anthology of women poets. She is a board member of the Marin Poetry Center, birdwatcher, yogini, mother, grandmother, chief cook and bottle-washer. In other words, an ordinary woman! Her first book, *The Daily Absurd*, was released in 2014.

Laurie Kolp, author of *Upon the Blue Couch* (Winter Goose Publishing, 2014) and *Hello, It's Your Mother* (Finishing Line Press, upcoming) is president of Texas Gulf Coast Writers and belongs to the Poetry Society of Texas. Laurie's poems have appeared in the 2015 *Poet's Market*, *Poeming Pigeons*, *Turtle Island Quarterly* and more. An avid runner and lover of nature, Laurie lives in Southeast Texas with her husband, three children and two dogs.

Linda Ferguson's work has been published in journals such as *VoiceCatcher Journal*, *The Santa Fe Literary Review*, *The Milo Review* and *Gold Man Review*. She's won many awards for her poetry and the *Perceptions* Magazine of the Arts Award for her lyric essay "Baila Conmigo." She also teaches creative writing and would like to be a ballerina when she grows up. <www.bylindaferguson.blogspot.com>

Linda Flaherty Haltmaier is an award-winning screenwriter and poet. She is the winner of the Homebound Publications Poetry Prize for 2015 and her poetry collection, *Rolling Up the Sky*, is forthcoming in February 2016. Her debut chapbook, *Catch and Release*, was published by Finishing Line Press in 2015. A Harvard graduate, Linda lives on Boston's North Shore with her husband and daughter, and walks the beach most days in search of blue sea glass and inspiration. <http://myconsumingpassions.blogspot.com>

Linda Hofke lives in Germany, where she writes, takes photographs, and puts her lead foot to use on the Autobahn. You can find her work at *iARTistas*, *Mouse Tales Press*, *Curio Poetry*, *Microw*, *Bolts of Silk*, and other online and print journals. She is a lazy blogger who sporadically posts at Lind-guistics.com.

Linda Jackson Collins is a former editor-in-chief of the Sacramento Poetry Center's poetry journal, *Tule Review*. Her own poems have appeared in *The Cape Rock*, *Late Peaches*, *Walrus*, *American River Review*, and elsewhere. She believes that when the ancients spoke of ambrosia, they were talking about avocados.

Lori Levy's poems have appeared in *Poet Lore*, *RATTLE*, *Nimrod International Journal*, and a variety of other literary journals in the U.S., England, and Israel. She published a bilingual (English/Hebrew) book of her poems in Israel, titled,

In the Mood for Orange. Though she now lives in Los Angeles, she grew up in Vermont, and lived in Israel for 16 years. Her two little grandchildren keep her on her toes and entertained. <avilori@yahoo.com>

Lori Loranger is a 35-year resident of rural Skamania County, on the Washington side of the Columbia River Gorge, where she practices mediation and meditation, does tai chi and drinks chai tea. Lori enjoys baking and eating a wide variety of pies. Her poetry appears in *Ghost Town Poetry* anthologies volume 1 and 2 (edited by Toni Partington and Chris Luna), and *Visions of Light* by Raymond Klein. Her poem "The Crow and I Wait for AAA" appeared in *Poeming Pigeons: Poems about Birds*. <lorangerlori@gmail.com>

Lu Pierro's poems have appeared, or are forthcoming in *Ars Poetica, Natural Awakenings, US1, Blast Furnace, If and Only If*, and *Threeandahalfpoint9, East Fork* among other journals. She is the recipient of the Dodge Foundation Scholarship and the Dorothy E. Laurence Scholarship from the Fine Arts Work Center in Provincetown, Mass. She lives in New Jersey with her husband and Mr. Tips her cat. She is currently working on a Noir novel about New Orleans.

Mariano Zaro has published four books of poetry: *Where From/Desde Donde, Poems of Erosion/Poemas de la erosión, The House of Mae Rim/La casa de Mae Rim* and *Tres letras/Three Letters*. He has translated American poets Philomene Long and Tony Barnstone. He earned a Ph.D. in Linguistics from the University of Granada (Spain). He currently teaches Spanish at Rio Hondo College (Whittier, CA). <www.marianozaro.com>

Mark L. Levinson was born ten miles from Boston and lives ten miles from Tel Aviv. For a time he blogged about technical writing, his occupation for many years, but recently he has concentrated more on Hebrew-to-English translation. He has spent a day as a TV quiz contestant, a day as a trash collector, a day as an encyclopedia salesman, and several as a film extra. He has a wife and son. <www.elephant.org.il/the-why-of-style>

Martie Odell-Ingebretsen has taken many classes in creative writing, poetry and fiction. Her Novella, *Sweet William*, was published in 2013. She has also written a number of short stories, and over two thousand poems, currently. Many of her poems have been published. She finds poetry to be a way to express her deepest feelings. She is a keen observer and finds imagery in all things, and in so doing appreciates the beauty and learns from the wisdom that surrounds her.

Mary Kay Rummel is Poet Laureate of Ventura County, California. Her seventh book of poetry, *The Lifeline Trembles*, was published by Blue Light Press as a winner of the 2014 Blue Light Award. *What's Left is the Singing* was also published by Blue Light Press. She frequently performs poetry with musicians. Retired from the University of Minnesota, she teaches part time at California State University, Channel Islands. <marykayrummel.com>

Matt Hohner, a Baltimore native, holds an M.F.A. in Writing and Poetics from Naropa University. His work has appeared in numerous publications, including *Free State Review*, *The Sow's Ear*, *The Potomac* and *Truck*. Hohner's chapbook *States* was published by Third Ear Books (1999). Hohner recently won and took third place in the 2015 Maryland Writers Association Poetry Prize. Hohner is a former high school English teacher and lives in Baltimore City with his wife and cat.

M.J. Iuppa lives on Red Rooster Farm near the shores of Lake Ontario. Most recent poems, lyric essays and fictions have appeared in the following journals: *Poppy Road Review*, *Digging to the Roots*, *Ealain*, *Poetry Pacific Review*, *100 Word Story*, *Avocet*, *Turtle Island Quarterly*, *Boyne Berries Magazine* (Ireland), *The Lake*, (U.K.); forthcoming in *Camroc Review*, *Tar River Poetry*, *Corvus Review*, *Clementine Poetry*, among others. She is the Director of the Visual and Performing Arts Minor Program at St. John Fisher College. <mjiuppa.blogspot.com>

Nathan Tompkins is a writer living in Portland, Oregon. His work has appeared in several publications including *NonBinary Review*, *Angle*, *North West Words*, *Keeping It Weird* (anthology), and others. Nathan is the author of two chapbooks, *Junk Mail of the Heart* and *The Dog Stops Here*.

Paul Belz is an environmental educator and writer based in Oakland, California. He develops and teaches natural history workshops for children, their parents, and their teachers. *Terrain Magazine*, the *East Bay Monthly*, *Childcare Exchange Magazine*, the website *Boots'n'All*, the organization *Oakland Wild*'s blog, and the blog *Green Global Travel* have published his articles. His poetry appears in a wide range of magazines. He is an enthusiastic backpacker and a world traveler.

Paulann Petersen, Oregon Poet Laureate Emerita, has six full-length books of poetry, most recently *Understory*, from Lost Horse Press in 2013. Her poems have appeared in many journals and anthologies, including *Poetry*, *The New Republic*, *Prairie Schooner*, *Willow Springs*, *Calyx*, and the Internet's *Poetry Daily*. She was a Stegner Fellow at Stanford University, and the recipient of the 2006

Holbrook Award from Oregon Literary Arts. In 2013 she received Willamette Writers' Distinguished Northwest Writer Award.

Penelope Scambly Schott's verse biography of Puritan dissident Anne Hutchinson, *A Is for Anne: Mistress Hutchinson Disturbs the Commonwealth*, received an Oregon Book Award. Other books about women in history include *Penelope: The Story of the Half-Scalped Woman* and *Lily Was a Goddess, Lily Was a Whore*. She lives in Portland and Dufur, Oregon where she teaches an annual poetry workshop.

Rachelle M. Parker is a Nassawadox born, Brooklyn bred girl. She now resides in eclectic Montclair, NJ. There she offers her stories and poems, which have appeared in *The Elohi Gadugi Journal* and *The Path Magazine*. She has been named the first prize winner of the Pat Schneider Poetry Contest 2014. The poem is forthcoming in their *Peregrine Journal*. She is a 2015 Callaloo Creative Workshop participant. <rachelleparker@outlook.com>

Richard King Perkins II is a state-sponsored advocate for residents in long-term care facilities. He lives in Crystal Lake, IL with his wife, Vickie and daughter, Sage. He is a three-time Pushcart nominee and a Best of the Net nominee. He has poems forthcoming in *The William and Mary Review*, *Sugar House Review*, *Free State Review*, *Plainsongs* and *Milkfist*. <roguesatellite@yahoo.com>

Rick Blum has been writing humorous essays and poetry for more than 25 years during stints as a nightclub owner, high-tech manager, market research mogul and, most recently, alter kaker. His poems have appeared in *Humor Times*, *Boston Literary Magazine*, *Hobo Pancakes*, and *Bohemia Journal*, among others. <rickpblum@verizon.net>

Robert R. Sanders has won over three dozen international awards in creative design, animation, and photography. He was nominated for an Emmy for *Fire Mountain*, a news documentary detailing the eruption of Mount. St. Helens. Robert's work spans half a century of creative development through an analog and digital journey. He's a teacher to thousands of aspiring artists, while always remaining a student of the light. \<RobertSandersPhoto.com>

Sarah Ghoshal teaches writing at Montclair State University, reads poetry when she should be grading, loathes most films made from books and loves Yankee baseball. She has two chapbooks, *Changing the Grid* (Finishing Line Press, 2015) and *The Pine Tree Experiment* (Lucky Bastard Press, 2015). Her poetry can also be found in *Arsenic Lobster*, *Winter Tangerine Review* and *Red Savina Review*, among others. She lives in New Jersey with her husband, her happy little baby, and their faithful dog, Comet. <www.sarahghoshal.com>

Shawn Aveningo is a globally published, award winning poet who can't stand the taste of coconut, eats pistachios daily and loves shoes ... especially red ones! Her work has appeared in over 80 literary journals & anthologies, including *poeticdiversity: the litzine of Los Angeles*, who recently nominated her work for a Pushcart. She is the co-founder of The Poetry Box® and web-designer for *VoiceCatcher: a journal of women's voices & visions*. Shawn is a proud mother of three and lives with her husband in Beaverton, Oregon. <redshoepoet.com>

Sreemoyee Roy Chowdhury is currently writing a PhD in English Literature at Durham University, UK, and holds the post of co-editor of the journal, *Postgraduate English*, a peer-reviewed academic journal. Sreemoyee writes poetry for catharsis and a genuine desire to engage with and understand the world around her. <sreemoyee.roy-chowdhury@durham.ac.uk>

Stephen McGuinness is 46 and works as a chef in Dublin, Ireland. He tries to write simple poetry, steeped in family life and in the city he loves. He has had some poems published in online journals. <www.facebook.com/pages/poetry-with-a-small-p/841525705869320>

Susan Mahan began writing poetry when her husband died in 1997. She served as an editor for *The South Boston Literary Gazette* from 2002-2010. She is a frequent reader at open mics and has written four chap books.

Susan Star Paddock is a family counselor living on a farm in Gettysburg, PA. She is a 70 year old gardener, community volunteer, and poet. Every year she, her husband and various grandchildren take tent camping trips through the national and state parks of the US. She's a vegetarian. <www.susanstarpaddock.com >

Suzanne Bruce, originally from Oklahoma, married her high school sweetheart. As military, they lived in 13 homes in 22 years settling in California. Her inspirations are the ocean and their Friday night tradition of pizza and champagne! Involved with poetry groups in the San Francisco Bay Area, her work has won several prizes and is published in numerous journals. Her book, *Voices Beyond the Canvas*(2007) is ekphrastic work with artist Janet Manalo. <www.ekphrasticexpressions.com>

Sylvia Riojas Vaughn's work once prompted a fellow writer to observe, "I think she's hungry." True, pickles, popcorn, and tamales have all found their way into her poems and plays. Her play, *La Tamalada*, was produced in Fort Worth. She's been published recently in *Triadæ Magazine*, *Somos en escrito Magazine*, and *The Great Gatsby Anthology*. <paul_sylvia@prodigy.net>

Tammy Robacker served as Poet Laureate of Tacoma, WA in 2010-11 and she is a 2011 Hedgebrook Writer-in-Residence award winner. Her poetry book, *Villain Songs*, is forthcoming (ELJ Publications, 2016). Her manuscript, *We Ate Our Mothers, Girls* was a finalist in the Floating Bridge Chapbook Contest. Tammy's poetry has appeared in *VoiceCatcher*, *Duende*, *WomenArts*, *Comstock Review* and *Cascadia Review*. Currently enrolled in the MFA program at Pacific Lutheran University, Tammy volunteers at CALYX Press and lives in Oregon. <www.pearlepubs.com>

Taylor Graham is a volunteer search-and-rescue dog handler in the Sierra Nevada. She's included in the anthologies *Villanelles* (Everyman's Library, 2012) and *California Poetry: From the Gold Rush to the Present* (Santa Clara University, 2004). Her latest book is *What the Wind Says* (Lummox Press, 2013), poems about living and working with her canine search partners over the past 40 years. <poetspiper@gmail.com>

Terri Niccum is a former journalist and special education teacher. She lives in Southern California where she continues to advocate for children with special needs. Her poetry has appeared in the anthologies *Grand Passion: The Poets of Los Angeles and Beyond* and *News From Inside*; and in *A.K.A. Magazine*; *Daybreak: Tsunami*, among others. Her chapbook, *Looking Snow in the Eye*, was published by Finishing Line Press. Niccum was selected as a semi-finalist for the 2014 Pablo Neruda Prize for Poetry. She is married to singer-songwriter Bob Niccum and together they make up two thirds of The Other Half, an eclectic vocal trio.

Tricia Knoll is a Portland, Oregon poet with average cooking skills, but she has tended a lush vegetable garden every growing season for more than 40 years. Her poetry has appeared widely in dozens of journals or anthologies. Two poems have been nominated for Pushcart prizes. Her chapbook, *Urban Wild*, is available from Amazon and Finishing Line Press. Late in 2015 *Ocean's Laughter* will be out from Aldrich Press. <triciaknoll.com>

Victorio Reyes is an activist and artist living in Albany, NY and holds and MFA degree from The Vermont College of Fine Arts. His poems have appeared in the

Acentos Review, The Mandala Journal, Mobius, and *Word Riot.* In 2014, Reyes served on a panel entitled "Uncovering Hip Hop Poetry" at the AWP Conference. Also, Reyes is a pigeon fan, having been raised around homing pigeons his entire life.

Index of Poets

The following poets whose poem(s) begin on the annotated page number(s) are indexed by last name:

Angier, Heather: 38
Aveningo, Shawn: 105
Belz, Paul: 46
Bloom, Irene: 99
Blum, Rick: 23
Bodin, Joanne S.: 42
Boyles, Jill: 112
Brown, Katy: 60
Bruce, Suzanne: 62
Burn, Jane: 32
Cain, Cathy: 110
Chowdhury, Sreemoyee Roy: 88
Colby, Joan: 59
Collins, Linda Jackson: 69
Duncan-O'Neal, Jan: 17
Easterly, Christine: 50
Feigenbaum, Laurel: 90
Ferguson, Linda: 16, 27
Ghoshal, Sarah: 92
Graham, Taylor: 68
Haag, Jan: 24
Haltmaier, Linda Flaherty: 19
Hofke, Linda: 113
Hohner, Matt: 87
Howells, Ann: 82
Howington, Georgette: 44
Huffman, A.J.: 21
Iuppa, M.J.: 117
Kerner, Helen: 102
Knoll, Tricia: 53, 67
Kolp, Laurie: 31
Kouwenhoven, Christine: 101

Laarif, Boutheina Boughnim: 29
Leotta, Joan: 66
Levinson, Mark L.: 58
Levy, Lori: 76
Loranger, Lori: 20
Mahan, Susan: 116
Martin, Carolyn: 93
McGuinness, Stephen: 71
McQueen, Debra: 30
Meier, Barbara A.: 114
Meltvedt, Deborah: 85
Merrifield, Karla Linn: 91
Morrison, JenniferAnne: 64
Moscoso, Elizabeth: 33
Niccum, Terri: 106
Odell-Ingebretsen, Martie: 98
Orosco, Dawn: 103
Paddock, Susan Star: 57
Parker, Rachelle M.: 49
Perkins, Richard King, II: 65
Petersen, Paulann: 15, 36
Pierro, Lu: 78
Post, Connie: 41
Privateer, Ann: 97
Raphael, Dan: 72
Reilly, JC: 52
Reyes, Victorio: 80
Robacker, Tammy: 37
Roberts, Jeannie E.: 108
Rummel, Mary Kay: 54
Savage, Claudia F.: 94, 107
Schott, Penelope Scambly: 39
Schug, Larry: 118
Simpson, Jane: 77
Skillman, Judith: 34
Stevens, Jeanine: 45
Suter, Beth: 111

Tompkins, Nathan: 26
Vaughn, Sylvia Riojas: 51
Viceroy, Andrew David: 70
Von Alst, Cassie: 73
Vrenios, Elizabeth: 55
White, Kimberly: 83
Yolen, Jane: 96
Zaro, Mariano: 47

About The Poetry Box®

The Poetry Box® was founded in 2011 by Shawn Aveningo & Robert R. Sanders, who whole-heartedly believe that every day spent with the people you love, doing what you love, is a moment in life worth celebrating. It all started out as our way to help people memorialize the special milestones in their lives by melding custom poems with photographic artwork for anniversaries, birthdays, holidays and other special occasions. Robert and Shawn expanded on their shared passion for creating poetry and art with the introduction of The Poetry Box® Book Publishing.

The book you now hold in your hands, *The Poeming Pigeon — A Literary Journal of Poetry,* evolved from the first issue (*Poeming Pigeons: Poems about Birds*) Each semi-annual issue will have a unique theme, with Homer, *The Poeming Pigeon* mascot, taking flight to deliver poems to poetry lovers across the globe. Details and submission guidelines can be found at www.ThePoemingPigeon.com.

As Robert and Shawn continue to celebrate the talents of their fellow artisans and writers, they now offer professional book design and publishing services to poets looking to publish their collections of poems and authors looking to publish novels, memoirs and creative non-fiction.

And as always, The Poetry Box® believes in giving back to the community. Each month a portion of all sales will benefit a different charity. For a complete list of the charities currently supported, please visit the Giving Back page on their website at www.ThePoetryBox.com.

Feel free to visit The Poetry Box® online bookstore, where you'll find more books including:

Keeping It Weird: Poems & Stories of Portland, Oregon

Verse on the Vine: A Celebration of Community, Poetry, Art & Wine

The Way a Woman Knows by Carolyn Martin

Of Course, I'm a Feminist! edited by Ellen Goldberg

Poeming Pigeons: Poems about Birds

and more ...

Order Form

Need more copies for friends and family? No problem. We've got you covered with two convenient ways to order:

1. Go to our website at www.thePoetryBox.com and click on Bookstore.

or

2. Fill out the order form. Email it to Shawn@thePoetryBox.com or mail it to: The Poetry Box®, 2228 NW 159th Pl, Beaverton, OR 97006.

Name: _____

Shipping Address: _____

_____

Phone Number: (____) _____

Email Address: _____@_____

Payment Method: __Cash __Check __PayPal Invoice __Credit Card

Credit Card #: _____ CCV _____

Expiration Date: _____ Signature: _____

The *Poeming Pigeon — Poems about Food* # of Copies: _____

x $15.00: _____

Plus Shipping & Handling: _____
($3 per book, or $7.95 for 3 or more books)

Order Total: _____

Thank You!

CPSIA information can be obtained
at www.ICGtesting.com
Printed in the USA
FSOW02n0933201015
12356FS

9 780986 330476